MY JOURNEY IN THE SHADOW OF "THE" KING"

...from Graceland to the Promised Land

Danny Vann

My Journey In The Shadow of "The King"
........From Graceland to the Promised Land

Unless otherwise indicated, Bible quotations are taken from NKJV at BibleStudyTools.com.

Edited by George Gierhardt, Brad Williams, and Cortney Kramer.

ISBN-13: 978-1096910879
ISBN-10: 109691087X

My Journey In The Shadow of "The King"
........From Graceland to the Promised Land

Contents

My Journey In The Shadow of "The King"
........From Graceland to the Promised Land

Acknowledgements

By God's Grace and Mercy, He has brought many people into my life that have helped me get to the place to write this book and share my story. I thank God for His inspiration, for my family, and everyone that has helped me along the way.

I am most grateful to my wife, Lena, who has both encouraged me, and challenged me, to produce the best parts of *Me* in the text of the following pages. She has truly been a gift from God.

Thanks to Billy Aemisegger for all your diligence and technical expertise.

Thanks to my friends, George Gierhardt, Brad Williams, and Noel Leaman for sharing your wisdom and skills.

Finally, thanks to Gordy Kukulis, Scott Peterson, and Cortney Kramer of Wellspring Lutheran Services. Your enthusiasm has meant a lot during all the ups and downs in this mission to help the children and adults that are traveling along similar paths to mine. I pray that this book will help comfort and encourage many of them.

My Journey In The Shadow of "The King"
........From Graceland to the Promised Land

Sometimes life just doesn't seem fair. You are going along day-to-day and then WHAM – something outside of your control changes everything! In my case, it was my parents…they got divorced…then my whole world changed forever.

This is the story of my journey from an early childhood of peace and joy – to chaos and ever-changing circumstances that initially seemed to make no sense to me at all. But through all the struggles, I had a feeling that there was a purpose for everything that happened to me, my siblings, and our family. In spite of all the pain and confusion, I sensed there must be a reason for it all. I never gave up hope that things would change – for the better – and at times they did. Even though they would never be the same as they once were, I kept moving along and would not allow myself to get bitter – or to become so angry that I just gave up trying to be good and follow God's way of doing things. Even if others around me were quitters and lied and cheated to get what they wanted – that didn't mean that it was okay for me to follow them and start doing bad things too! I knew that I would have to answer for my own actions – I couldn't blame others for the things that "I" was doing. And I wanted and firmly believed that with God's help, if I put my mind and faith on something, I could accomplish it if I worked hard enough at it. And I did!!! I had dreams of my own that nobody could take from me. Those dreams, my love for God, and my music kept me going when others gave up, settled for less, or just shut down.

In the following pages you will see my journey from a broken home, to an orphanage, foster home, blended and broken family, to an emancipated minor and finally independence: continually striving to become a premiere Elvis impersonator. I even performed in Las Vegas and the Palace of Auburn Hills and was inducted into the Elvis Presley Impersonators International Hall of Fame. Additionally, I went on to become a family man and even an ordained minister, all the while I was keeping BOTH the "King of Rock-n-Roll" and the "King of Kings" in my sights. In spite of all the chaos and pain, I actually discovered that *it was fun being me*! Read on to see why I was able to turn out so positive – and not fall into the "poor-me" trap like many of those who traveled along a journey like mine.

If you are struggling with life – don't give up. You are NOT ALONE! Reach out to God. He listens, and He answers those who seek Him with all their heart.

My Journey In The Shadow of *"The King"*
........From Graceland to the Promised Land

Foreword by Gordon R. Kukulis

Danny's story is one of hope and resilience. It describes his struggles growing up, his successes in the world of music, his personal struggles in relationship with others, and his ultimate redemption and discovery of a cherished life. This book is not a roadmap for others, nor a cautionary tale. It presents as an honest account of his years to the present, un-varnished except for his wide-eyed exuberance for optimism, as identified by his 'glass half-full, and needing to be filled to the top' outlook on life.

Evident in his writing is the hope Danny has developed in life through his faith. Despite the chaos he endured in his formative years, Danny was encouraged to pursue, and at many critical times relent to, the higher power of his Savior. This encouragement came not only from close members of his family of origin, but through the kindness of strangers that he came to see as having been placed in his path by divine intervention.

From faith to hope, Danny has been driven to propel his life forward to success. Faith is the 'hand-in-glove' partner of resilience. Resilience is the outward expression of inner faith. Faith in himself, for Danny, was born of and nurtured by the unconditional love that he was blessed with by his maternal grandmother, Josie, and in a much less-consistent manner by his parents.

Understanding the events of Danny's early life as he experienced them, it is un-surprising that he reached out 'to pay it forward' to the boys in residential care at Lutheran Home. He was driven by his resilience to infuse that spirit, that faith in oneself, into the boys whose lives mirrored a time in his own life of need for support and interest from an unsolicited source. He marshaled his love, his talents, and his connections with others to provide evenings of fun and examples of the type of success within their grasps by accepting the unconditional love of others to foster their own self-beliefs. Danny's actions were a blessing to our program.

As Danny's life has progressed from those early days in his careers of business and music, his many ups and downs have altered his original visions of success. Though he has reached heights in both fields that few people ever do, his health has factored in as a major detour to the pinnacles he once had in mind. Despite this, I believe that Danny has arrived at his Graceland. His life will continue to unfold with new adventures and opportunities for him to share his talents, his faith, and his love for others. This book stands as a great touchpoint in that process. I thank him for sharing his story with all of us and for calling me 'friend'.

Gordy

Gordon R. Kukulis

Former Director of Lutheran Home,a residential treatment program of Lutheran Child & Family Service of Michigan

My Journey In The Shadow of "The King"
........From Graceland to the Promised Land

What can a simple handshake, a gallon of ice cream, a new shirt, or a pair of gloves do to change the world? Plenty if your world has been shaken to its core, and you are a child living in an orphanage or a foster home. In Michigan alone there are over 13,000 children living in the foster care system. What if YOU could make a difference for even ONE of those kids? You might not know it, but something as simple as a plaque of the Golden Rule or a set of Hot Wheels could help mold the attitude of impressionable teenagers for the rest of their life! No matter which side of this story you can relate to, the events really happened. Sometimes, the smallest things that people do for others, make the largest impact in the lives of those receiving these blessings. I know this to be true, because I am one of those children who has been blessed by others in many amazing ways!

This is my story – in my own words – and done in MY style of writing. I am NOT an English major – or an advanced college graduate. I hope the contents of this book will impact you and anyone needing to be encouraged about the things life puts in our path. Throughout this story, you will also see God's guidance at every stage of my life.

I have taken the liberty to change some names and places in order to respect people's privacy.

My Journey In The Shadow of "The King"
........From Graceland to the Promised Land

As far back as I can remember I always wanted to be like Elvis. As a pre-teen, in the 1960's my favorite time of week was to go grocery shopping with Mom because she would always buy me a new Elvis album. The more albums I heard, the more I wanted to sing like Elvis and get my own guitar. I was imitating Elvis as a little kid and well before my voice changed. I remember going to my friend Claude's house and singing into his dad's reel-to-reel tape recorder. I was crushed when Claude's voice changed and became very deep before my voice changed. But God knew the plans he had for me – there were great things on the horizon both professionally and personally. Imagine living your dream by performing in Las Vegas – or singing in front of 10,000 people at the Palace of Auburn Hills!!! By God's grace, I have done those things and more!!!

Hello – my name is Danny Vann. I am the oldest of six kids born to Jerry & Babe V. in Bay City, Michigan. Born in 1953, I am a Baby Boomer but, not a traditional one by any stretch. Most of my friends were Beatles, Stones, Rare Earth, Who or Chicago fans. I am, and always have been, a huge ELVIS fan. My Mom was 16 when I was born. By the time she was 22, she had **6** kids. Just five years later, she was divorced at 27. My two brothers and three sisters and I lived in several different relatives' homes and an orphanage. We were nearly adopted out of the foster homes that we were placed in all before I reached the age of 15!

My Journey In The Shadow of "The King"
........From Graceland to the Promised Land

This is the story of how I went from an orphanage to become a singer in Las Vegas – and at the same time from a teenage ice cream salesman to mid-level executive in corporate America. BUT, my primary goal in life was to be like Elvis – I wanted my own Graceland! Yet, God wasn't going to let me get too far off course. During the same time period I also went from altar boy to Eastern-meditating-disciple – and back to Christ again to become an ordained minister who was bound for glory in the Promised Land! It is my hope and prayer that through the pages of this book, you will be encouraged to see how I went from dis-grace to Graceland and from poverty to a successful career in corporate America. I also studied and followed God's Word and began traveling the route to the Promised Land. Even though there were many hard times, I kept my faith in God. I never gave up the hope that there was a reason things were happening to me when and where they did. As I got older, I began to see a pattern in my past. As bad as things seemed to get, I always came through them, and usually things got better for me in some way. I hope my life's journey will encourage you to keep your eye on God and trust in Him. You too can attain peace and joy no matter what your circumstances. God has plans for you – to prosper you and not harm you (Jeremiah 29:11). It's His promise.

My Journey In The Shadow of "The King"
........From Graceland to the Promised Land

From the time my siblings and I were young children, God and music were both very important in our early formative years. We went to Catholic Church on Sundays – and we all attended Catechism too, except Dad who never participated. Grandma Josie (my mom's mother) used to come to church with us at times, and she loved to sing those old gospel hymns! She and I had a *very* special relationship (I was her first grandson) – I loved hearing her sing and she loved me incredibly. I mean she just spoiled me something rotten. I loved it – and I loved her. I can't say that I remember ever seeing her read the Bible, but she always had one around. Grandma just loved people in general. She was Italian – Sicilian to be exact.

There were always lots of family and friends at Grandma's house during every holiday. It seemed for a while that we were at Grandma's house every weekend. There was always a lot of activity there since she had eight kids of her own. It was a fun time – hanging out with all my aunts and uncles and dozens of cousins. My Uncle Mike, Grandma's last child, was a year *younger* than me, so we practically grew up together. He was the same age as my brother Joe, and the three of us were inseparable . . . until I got my first guitar.

The holidays were the grandest gatherings of them all. All the Italian relatives would meet at Grandma's house and make homemade ravioli, bread, salads and lots of desserts. There would be hundreds of little pillows of dough-filled with the meat-spinach centers all over the house. I mean if there was a flat surface, tables, TV, radiators, stereo or anything horizontal, it had a white cotton sheet or clean towel on it and it was covered with drying raviolis. It seemed like Grandma was feeding an army with the pots and pots of red sauce and multiple loaves of fresh homemade bread. She'd get all the food ready – we'd go to church and when we got home....oh-boy! Mangia-mangia

My Journey In The Shadow of "The King"
........From Graceland to the Promised Land

(eat-eat) was the encouraging cry from Grandma's kitchen. The house was full of delicious smells and happy uplifting music! After we all ate until we were going to burst, and the women cleaned up the kitchen, all the adults would gather around the table and play cards for hours on end while we kids would play ball or ride our bikes around the neighborhood. We even got to watch Grandma's new console color TV (ours was still just a black and white set). The holiday movies were awesome in living color! It was a very special time and we all felt safe and happy at Grandma's.

But life wasn't all parties, pasta and bread there either. After Grandpa B died in 1957, Grandma got remarried and her new husband was a very heavy drinker. Sometimes he would go on 2-to-3 day drunken binges. Luckily, he was pretty happy in those early years. He just loved my sister Janet – he called her *Kisses*. And of course, he would always ask her to give him a kiss, then he would give her a quarter. It seemed he cared about her like Grandma cared about me.

Grandma was a steady figure in my life, I still remember Grandma going to church every Sunday. She always listened to music on the radio and on Sundays, it was the Polka hour – yes, Italians listen to Polka music, at least we did at Grandma's house. But Grandma and I would also sit out on her front porch and listen to the old County Music shows for hours. I loved to sing along and so did she. One of our favorites was *Your Cheatin' Heart* by Hank Williams. This was one of the first few songs I learned to play later in life after I finally got my first guitar.

As I look back on it now, it's amazing how much impact little moments like those can have on your life – and stick with you when you grow older. I can also remember all my (teenage) aunts and uncles coming and going while we listened to the "new" Motown hits on the radio. Sometimes they would join in and actually act out the words of the song *Dancing in the Streets* – what fun times we all had back then. Family time was just a natural thing – people spending time together and doing things together and caring about one another.

My Journey In The Shadow of "The King"
........From Graceland to the Promised Land

Grandma actually owned and drove the NEW 1965 Mustang Convertible back then. She was a lead-foot granny too. Every once in a while we'd ride along with Grandma to the local party store to get some refreshments like pop and beer (This was before the big department store outlets took over neighborhood Mom and pop stores) – other times we also went with Mom and Grandma to the bingo.

Later in life, I wound up writing a special song for Grandma that captured all of this. Here's the intro to it: "*Grandma's Song Intro*"[1] Of course, I called it "*Grandma's Song - Ode to Josie.*" To hear the songs, click the link or go to www.broadjam.com/songs/DannyVann

Life was pretty good in those early days, but with all the good things happening back then, there were also fights and arguments going on at granny's house between her and her new husband Grandpa Cherry. There were even fights between him and her kids (my aunts and uncles). In his later years, he got very mean when he drank. He would start yelling at everybody and throw things across the room, and at times even Janet would start crying. It was both confusing and stressful. How could such a nice guy turn so mean so quickly? Mom would gather us up and we would head back home, usually in silence, because of all the chaos we had just escaped. Luckily, those incidents were few and far between.

Like Elvis, I always enjoyed and was very comforted being around the church. In fact, at a very early age I felt called to become a "man of the cloth." This kind of disturbed me because I also always felt like I wanted to have children and have a "normal" married life. Those were mutually exclusive lifestyles to a young Catholic boy – because priests cannot be married. So, I had some confusion about those thoughts in my young adult years. I prayed about it and it seemed that I could actually *see* the children that I had in my future. I was also drawn at an early age to a magazine article of a man staring up looking into the stars with the moon over his shoulder. The caption read – "Do you wonder about the power of the universe?" I clipped the article and carried it with me for many years – it was an ad for the study of Rosicrucian's. I sent away for the starter kit once and learned that theirs was a lifelong study that required regular payments that never seemed to end. I was disappointed; it looked like a scam to me, so I tossed the material and turned my focus on music and ultimately on starting a family. However, the marriage and family pattern that I was being shown by my family was causing me confusion.

Back in the early 1960's, there was really nothing special about any of us – we were a struggling family that was trying to exist on a single income. Dad worked at the General Motors plant and made a decent living, but that only went so far with six kids and two adults. He had served in the Navy during the Korean War and married Mom when he got out. They had been raised in the same neighborhood and had mutual friends. When they got married, they initially lived in a Quonset hut (metal domed apartment) in the South End of Bay City, Michigan. But, when I was 3-4 years old, they bought the house over on the West side where we grew up. My youngest sister still owns it today. Our house was just a two-story, three bedroom, box-shaped home built around the early 1900's.

At first, we had a fairly *Leave it to Beaver* style life – Mom even walked me to school on my first day. Those were peaceful and *very* happy days for me. My favorite time at elementary school was MUSIC – of course. Mrs. Donnelly would gather us all around the piano and we would sing *America the Beautiful* and the *Star Spangled Banner*. Those were the days when we said the Pledge of Allegiance and had a morning prayer. The absolute best times came around St. Patrick's Day when Mrs. D would get out all her Irish tunes and we sang for what seemed like hours: *Too-Ra-Loo-Ra-Loo-Ral* (That's An Irish Lullaby), *Cockles and Mussels*, *H-A-R-R-I-G-A-N*, *Danny Boy* (My favorite – just kidding) and many more. Even back then, I just loved to sing!

I had my first girlfriend in the first grade - Kelley O'Riley. Like Charlie Brown's dream girl, she was a little red-haired girl with freckles. I used to sing her name in the old Irish song – "She's my dear, my darling one. Her eyes are sparkling full of fun....no other – no other – can take her place." I was in love, but of course, when word got out about us, the playground was abuzz with the news. The other kids made fun of us and held a mock wedding. And alas, my heart was broken (not for the last time) - Kelley would have nothing more to do with me. I remember Mom made some of my favorite soup and I was better in no time.

I had my first shot at stardom at Trombley Elementary School. They needed a dog barking sound for the school play and I was able to bark like our dog (Blacky) – so I got the part. People swore there was a real dog in school. OK, I know Elvis "sang" at a talent show....give me a few more years here, I'll get to it.

Life was going along pretty well for us, and with six kids under the age of seven, Mom really had her hands full. Since I was the oldest, I was taught all of the major duties; I learned to change the other babies' diapers before I was five. I also helped with cleaning, ironing, washing dishes, and watching the babies as needed. I guess you could say I was Mom's right-hand man from the ripe old age of four! Dad worked a lot of hours and at times he was on different shifts – sometimes working all night (3rd shift). But, when he finally got some time off, Dad liked fishing and would take us with him from time to time. The most exciting time was in the dead of winter when we went "ice" fishing. Grandpa V. would actually drive his car out on the ice at the mouth of the bay (hey – we're in Bay City – remember), and we would set up an ice shanty and sit in the cold and fish for hours. We sure caught a lot of perch and pan fish out of those waters.

Dad also liked to load us all up in the VW van (mini-bus) and drive all around Michigan to explore a lot. Before he moved to Florida, he boasted about a map of Michigan where he traced his excursions over nearly every road in the state that he had driven on at one time or another. This map was covered with red and blue pencil lines – he really had driven on almost every highway and dirt road in the entire state of Michigan. I guess that's where I got my sense of adventure from. Because, starting in my late teens, I traveled an average of 40,000 miles per year doing entertaining and other activities.

My Journey In The Shadow of "The King"
........From Graceland to the Promised Land

Overall, it seemed like Dad's favorite pastime was being out in the yard when the weather was warmer. He loved gardening and planting things. Dad had a real honest-to-goodness green thumb. I saw him stick things in the ground and watch them grow. I didn't know how he did it – until I had a home of my own and he finally shared his secret – Upstart root starter. He would take a cutting off a tree or bush and soak it for a week or two in a bucket (galvanized - not plastic) until it had little root shoots at the bottom. Then he'd stick it in the ground and water it daily – and presto, he'd have a new plant growing in the yard. I also enjoyed, and still enjoy, working the ground and watching things grow. We had a huge yard - nearly half an acre which was pretty good-sized for a home inside the city limits. Dad would hire a local farmer to plow the back half under during the spring and we would plant a huge vegetable garden. It was truly a family plot – we ALL helped pick out stones and weeds and then we planted all kinds of good stuff to eat. We had tomatoes, cucumbers, onions, radishes, cabbages, green peppers, beets, peas, corn, squash and more. Mom became an expert canner and our pantry was always full of a rainbow of colors shining out from those glass mason jars. We had a huge stand-up freezer too. Dad would take us berry picking for strawberries in the spring and huckleberries (blueberries) in the late summer. I remember also climbing up and down the huge drainage ditches on the outskirts of Bay City picking wild asparagus. Imagine the scene – you're a farmer tending your crops and up pulls this VW van. Six kids and two adults jump out and start crawling up and down all the drainage ditches along your field. I can't tell you how many mucky "soakers" I got slip-sliding at the bottom of those springtime murky man-made creeks. I learned quite a lesson from Dad – there's food all over if you know where to look and how to find it. We would also go on wild mushroom hunts and wild berry hunts – anything to help feed the large crew on a factory worker's budget.

These were the early days of Elvis' movie career, too. Mom was a huge Elvis fan – and she watched ALL the Elvis movies. She had dozens of Elvis records – 45's and LP's (Long Playing). Believe it or not, one of my favorite pastimes was going shopping with Mom, because she always let me buy the newest Elvis album! We would both rush home, put on the new Elvis music and listen and dance while we put away the groceries. There was just something about hearing Elvis music that lifted our hearts – and it still does. He sure had a way of energizing every song he sang.

Yes, life was quite an adventure back then. I remember the very first time I got my name in the paper – it wasn't for singing though. Along with our large yard, we had a lot of trees. There were a half dozen apple trees, a pear tree, several peach and plum trees, an apricot tree and several huge maple trees. Well, as kids with all those trees, you know there was a lot of climbing going on. And as the oldest, I just *had* to always go the highest of anybody.

One day, I was kind of bugged by my little brother Joe always following me wherever I went, and I wanted to be alone for a change. When he wouldn't leave me alone, I decided I would climb the giant maple tree. I mean this tree was HUGE – way over 50 feet tall – and I was determined to out-climb my brother and get up so high that I could hang out all day and not be bothered. Well, I sure got my wish that day; I shinnied up a large branch and wound up 20-25 feet in the air. (I know Mom would have killed me if she saw me climbing that high.) I think I was higher than the house; I could see all of the roof from my vantage point. Anyway, going up was one thing – I had a pursuer that I was determined to leave behind. I made it up to a comfy area where the tree trunk splint into a large Y. I sat in the saddle of those two branches and enjoyed my freedom for quite a while, but when I finally decided to come down out of the tree, that's when I discovered that I was in trouble – BIG trouble. There were no little nubs or branches for my feet on the way down - I was STUCK 20+ feet straight up in the air in this huge maple tree. It was way beyond Dad's tallest ladder and nobody was around that could help me down. Luckily, Dad was at work, so they called the fire department and, of course, the newspaper reporters showed up too. I was never so embarrassed in my whole life (I was 10 at the time). Well, the next day my name was in the paper for the fire rescue – Danny V playing "Tarzan" in the local trees.

My Journey In The Shadow of "The King"
........From Graceland to the Promised Land

We were one big happy family --- at least that's what I thought until my parents started having frequent arguments. Then the marital disagreements escalated into full body contact brawls. Unlike the loving home life portrayed in Elvis' life, at my house there were many, many arguments. Being Italian, and having to defend herself against the violence of a man a full head taller than her, Mom would grab anything nearby to throw at Dad - we *literally* had tossed salads frequently in our house. Unfortunately, we also had a lot of broken doors, walls, telephones, and other things that got in the way of Dad's furious path. That's when Mom began shooing us kids upstairs and locking the door that sealed the stairwell connected to the dining room. On the outside, it had one of those sliding bolts that you slide and then fold up or down. We would sit on the steps and listen to all the screaming and hear the slapping of flesh against flesh. You could hear the thumps and the sound of furniture moving and dishes breaking. This would go on for what seemed like hours. It was heartbreaking for us kids. How could parents get so angry with each other and behave like this? We all cried out and tried to calm each other, but nothing we did on our own could really help us while we listened to the pain being inflicted on the other side of that door. Mom would threaten to call the police; then Dad would rip the phone off the wall. Then all of sudden you would hear the front door open and everything would go quiet. We were ALL ALONE in the house – locked upstairs. The feelings of despair and worry caused the younger kids to cry and weep while us older ones would try to comfort them. It was a time of emptiness in our hearts wondering how our parents could be so mean to each other. Why were they doing this to each other? How could they leave us alone like this? When would they return home? There was no bathroom upstairs and there were a couple of times when the younger kids had to go so bad...well let's just say an accident happened and it required cleanup when we got out. Over time, we discovered that if we kicked at the door over and over and over again, sometimes the slide bolt would jostle itself loose and we could free ourselves before anybody got back. One time in the summer, my brother Joe, jumped out of the 2nd floor window and came into the dining room to let us out.

This arguing routine went on for quite some time and then one night Dad woke me up a little after midnight when he got home from work. "Daniel – Dan. Wake up. Your mom's gone and I need to go find her. Come downstairs and stay by the phone until I get back."

"Okay Dad", I said. That was the first sign of the ultimate outcome. Then the divorce hit and Dad moved out. It ripped our world apart. It was a nasty breakup. Mom was really angry and we kids were all confused and mad that our dad left us. We all felt abandoned and lost now that our family was being ripped apart. It was all like a bad dream. We went through the motions every day, but after school we returned home to ongoing sadness, chaos and uncertainty.

Then we were sent to stay at different relatives homes on-and-off, while Mom tried to deal with finances and bills. This was not a good job situation for a single Mom in the early 1960's. There were times when, as the oldest, I was depended on to be the man of the house. I was eleven, and I literally had to run the household while Mom was away at work. Oh, we had official babysitters, but they couldn't control all six of us. I usually had to get involved somehow. By the time I was 12, the job was all mine. In spite of it all, I always knew God was there – watching over me and all the kids. I believed He existed and that He had a special place in His heart for kids. I have always been a glass half-full (not empty) kind of guy. Dad always told me "You can do whatever you put your mind to" – and I believed him. Somehow, I just knew if I believed in something, I could make it happen. Later I learned that God honors faith, especially when it's directed at Him and through Him. I still had my dreams of being a professional singer someday. In middle school, after waiting many years, I finally made my own "guitar" out of a cigar box, a broom handle, and rubber bands.

My Journey In The Shadow of "The King"
........From Graceland to the Promised Land

Then, Mom married a sailor. He was a guitar player and I thought I was in heaven. I watched him play for hours. One of his favorite songs was *This Diamond Ring*. He played it over and over for me; we had a blast together. Unfortunately, their marriage was very short-lived and he left us after less than a year. Life changed for the worse after that. We wound up living on Korean War surplus foods like powdered eggs, powdered milk and super-hard surplus brick cheese. I remember being so angry and depressed that I locked myself in our old garage and threatened to kill myself. I really would have never done it, I just needed someone to notice *me* and understand that I was really in pain.

Being on our own during the day was hard. We got into trouble several times, and we destroyed several of the out-buildings in the back of our property. We never had any major trouble though; nothing with the law. The house became overrun with rats, and we would see them running across the floor when we watched TV at night. Things were getting worse and worse. How were we going to get by on all this? Even though Mom seemed to take it all in stride, she decided we would be better off in an orphanage where they would feed us three meals a day and clothe us. At the time, I was the oldest and even *I* wore hand-me-downs.

My Journey In The Shadow of "The King"
........From Graceland to the Promised Land

Figure 1 My brother Joe and me at St. Vincent Home in Saginaw

I was 12 when we first walked up the seemingly giant 10 steps to the enormous brick mansion called St. Vincent's Home in Saginaw, Michigan. In spite of the fact that they split us kids up, boys and girls on different sides of the building, we were quite happy to be there. We all got brand new clothes.

The food was pretty good, and they ALWAYS had great desserts. It was a Catholic institution and was run by Dominican Nuns – Daughters of Charity. They were fairly strict, but they had BIG hearts for the kids; especially the kids that were well behaved. Of course, since I was already a miniature adult, I seemed to fit right in and quickly became a favored child (God was definitely with us at this place) – we all continued our Catechism classes and wound up receiving our First Communion while at St. Vincent's.

My Journey In The Shadow of *"The King"*
........*From Graceland to the Promised Land*

I have to admit that it was lonely at times without Mom and my whole family gathering together like we used to do. I heard that my little sisters were often crying at night as they went to bed. We were all in a whirlwind of constant change, and even though this was a "good" change, it still took its toll on our hearts and minds. As the oldest, I felt like I had to help all my brothers and sisters through these things, and so I was always talking to them and comforting them in every way I could. The good portion for us was that we were surrounded by loving caring, and spiritual nuns and counselors who were trained to handle kids going through life-changing circumstances.

After some time, we all adapted to our new way of life. I even became an altar boy while I was there and literally went to church every day of the week, and twice on Sunday. It was quite an ordeal to see all of the kids gather every morning for church service called *Mass*. There were a couple of orphan brothers that always sat together and usually got into trouble of some sort – I think they were the Mueller Brothers. Anyway, every time the priest would burn incense, one of the brothers would hold his breath because he hated the smell. Without fail, he would pass out, and we would hear the clunking of his head as his limp body fell between the old wooden pews. Of course, the Sisters (nuns) would quickly rush over, pick him up, and carry him out of church. The rest of us would giggle and try not to be seen, or else we might get a swat for acting up in church. I don't remember too many other problems, although I had to have a talk with some of the others boys to make sure they left my brothers and sisters alone and didn't bully them when I wasn't around. But, overall, it was a good experience there for us – not like you see on some of the TV movies where orphaned kids are running wild and beating each other up. We were highly supervised and always had something to do to keep us busy.

As I learned the stories of how some of the other kids wound up at the Home, I was heartbroken. It kind of shook me up at times, but I would always try to encourage them and say, "Well at least now you have good food, new clothes, and people that care about you here."

My Journey In The Shadow of "The King"
........From Graceland to the Promised Land

We were disappointed at times when no one showed up for visitation weekends. It made us feel totally abandoned by our family. I learned early in life that you just have to keep hanging in there because things would always change somehow. The nuns also were very encouraging – constantly smiling and ready at a moment's notice to listen whenever we wanted to talk (or cry) about our situation. They also encouraged us to pray and talk to God about things that bothered us.

I didn't realize it at the time, but God was very present in all of my life events. You'll see that as we take this trip together. I know now that He is always with every one of us – watching us like a doting parent, pulling for us at every turn. If you are a parent or grandparent, you know what I'm talking about. You want the best for your kids. When they are brand new babies, you hover over them at every moment. You pamper them and wash and sterilize everything. I'm here to tell you that God is like that with each and every one of us. I'm reminded of Psalm 139:16, *"Your eyes saw my unformed body. All the days ordained for me were written in Your book before one of them came to be."* God is a very loving and caring Father; I'll prove it as you read on.

In the summer of 1965, St. Vincent's owned a villa out in the country that was a moderate-sized mini-farm with a huge swimming pool, horses, a couple of large dormitories, and a Chapel. Once school was out, we were all moved out there for the whole summer. It was, and still is, located about 15 miles west of Saginaw in Shields Township. It was great to get out of the city and have a change of scenery. We had plenty of space to run and play and stretch our legs while playing games and swimming. Even though we had some light chores, it was like a perpetual vacation. We were quite fortunate because they also had counseling, so we were able to vent a lot and get some Christian perspective on what was happening in our lives. I can't speak for all my brothers and sisters, but this was very helpful to me personally. I remember the boy's counselor, Brother John. He was a very gentle man and spent hours walking and talking to us about life and God's plan for us all. It was helpful to hear him explain that there was hope for us in the long run. Talking through things eased my mind and actually helped me sleep better at night. He also led the Bible studies.

My Journey In The Shadow of "The King"
........From Graceland to the Promised Land

We had some great priests, too; Father Francis was like a big teddy bear with all the kids. He was very friendly and outgoing. I remember how hairy he was; he looked like a monk with his brown-hooded robe with the white rope-like cord tied around his big belly. He was a solid father figure to many of us as he made his way around the grounds and during meals and gatherings. He corrected us, prayed with us and even cried with some of us. It was comforting to see him with his peaceful attitude showing up day after day. The stability of his presence helped fill the void of our missing parents and family.

Then there were the Sisters; Sister Dorothy was my favorite. She tried to be very stern but always seemed to crack a smile when she was correcting us. She was a slender woman with mouse-like features. I think she was Irish, and she had bright white teeth. She just had the most uplifting personality of all of them, and I was really comfortable being around her. She always seemed to be humming or singing something. Of course, with my bent on music, we cliqued right away! By spending so much time with them every day, I learned that all the clergy were just plain old people like you and me, and so were the volunteers from the Knights of Columbus. These folks were always cheerful and happy to see all us kids. They would show up with pickup trucks full of goodies donated by local merchants – cookies, cakes, ice cream – you never knew what the next load was going to bring. But, we always knew it was going to be GOOD! I don't remember the exact headcount of all the kids with me during our stay at the home, but I would guess it was in excess of 50 kids. If you've ever had a birthday party for your own kids, you know what it's like to have even 10 kids running around a house. Imagine trying to watch and control over 50!! It took a lot of helpers, volunteers, and activities to keep us in line and run us until we were tired out enough to get to sleep at night, especially in those open room dorms with all the beds lined up and down the aisles. Yet, somehow they did it, night after night. I couldn't help thinking about being back "home" in our own bedrooms. It would be a while before that would happen, but we would be the fortunate ones. Most of the kids would never see their old homes again.

My Journey In The Shadow of "The King"
........From Graceland to the Promised Land

It was during this time that we found out that Mom had moved out of town and was now several hours away from us. Once again we all felt abandoned by our mom and dad, even though we were surrounded by caring church people; that was no replacement for our own family and our own home. It was a weird feeling to realize that the Sisters and Counselors at St. Vincent's Home were now officially "our family." God does indeed work in mysterious ways.

One of the most impressive things that happened to me while we were at the Home occurred in the fall of that year back in the city, when a local band came to entertain for all of us kids. I was blown away – live musicians performing for *me*. Then the most incredible thing happened! After their mini-concert, they came off the stage and met with each one of us! **They shook my hand!** That impressed me so much that later in my music career, I also jumped off the stage at ALL my concerts and would call the kids up front and shake all their hands, too. That day in the orphanage - - - one simple loving handshake turned into 10,000's of handshakes over 40+ years that I have been doing Elvis all over Michigan! And I can't begin to tell you how many young adult men and women have come up to me over the years and exclaimed how impressed they were that *I* shook *their* hand when they were just a kid. People, one act of random kindness **really can** change the world! The things you do to others really do come back to you – sometimes many years later – but what you do will absolutely impact others in some way. It's up to you whether it is good or not.

D uring the second year at the orphanage, we were split up even more as we were gradually sent out two-by-two to several different foster homes back in Bay City. At first, since I was older, I wound up alone at my foster home until my little brother Bobby fell ill at the foster home he was sent to and they returned him to St. Vincent's Home. When he was nursed back to good health, the case workers decided to send him over to stay with me and my foster family. This was a pretty trying time for all of us kids, because we were constantly being challenged by adjusting to new families, changing schools, and making new friends. There was a constant hounding loneliness (or hole in our hearts) because we all missed our parents and extended family.

The foster family I had was fabulous. Mrs. Mulcahey had the patience of a saint; nothing ever seemed to faze her. About the only time I ever saw her upset was when one of us kids was upset. My little brother cried on many weekends when nobody showed up to pick us up for parental visits. I'm not sure exactly what happened to my parents during this time, but the visits from them were hit-and-miss at times. We went through this for a year or so. When I was able to talk with the other kids, they all said they wished things would get back to normal. Even though we were with new families, it wasn't the same. We were all still lonely for each other! I missed seeing my siblings and getting together with them.

I still felt responsible for all of them, so I took a job as an ice cream boy – walking through the streets of Bay City pushing one of those white freezer

Figure 2: Ice cream push cart like I used at my foster home

carts. I can still hear those goofy bells ringing and ringing. Sometimes I would sing a song to the beat of the ringing bells. It was a lot of walking, but I wouldn't trade the experience or memories of it for anything. That summer I saved all my money and bought each of my brothers and sisters a used bike – so we could at least ride around the city and see each other.

It was a very stressful time in my life, but I never lost my hope and the dream that I would be a singer and get a guitar someday. I made some friends in the neighborhood and would sing for them whenever I got the chance. I didn't have a guitar yet, so I usually just sang along with the radio or whenever somebody would listen to me acapella. It was nice having some new friends, but I still missed my brothers and sisters and my family during that time.

Then I heard that my sister Janet might be adopted by her foster family. I panicked – *what was happening to us*? What could *I* do about it? *Would I ever see her again?* I made an appointment with the Catholic Family Services case worker and was told that only my parents could change things. I cried out to God, "How could You let this happen?"

My Journey In The Shadow of "The King"
........From Graceland to the Promised Land

I felt my hope slipping away; the situation was looking very grim from where I sat. I felt confused and helpless. Then, out of nowhere, my dad came to visit and explained that he had raised the money to get the house back, and he was fixing it up so he could get us all back home again. The adoption was on hold! Wow! This was like a miracle for us!!! God truly hears the prayers of His children. I was always willing to believe prayer could and would help whatever situation came my way. This helped my faith grow even stronger!

Keeping my faith helped me get through many depressing events in my life. I also prayed for my family whenever things looked hopeless. This was something my Grandma Josie encouraged and was also taught in our catechism classes when we were growing up. Now I could also start praying thankful prayers to God for this sudden and very positive turn of events in our lives! Our lives perked up and energy levels increased with this good news. Hope was restored and we could finally look forward to what was going to happen next in our lives. God is good!

My Journey In The Shadow of "The King"
........*From Graceland to the Promised Land*

I t took Dad a while, but eventually he got my brother Bob and me out of our foster home and somehow stopped the adoption process of my sister. It was an awesome adventure living back home with Dad. We had him all to ourselves. We would go to school, and I'd watch Bob when we came home for about half an hour or so – until Dad got home. Then we'd work for hours fixing things in the house, building new walls, and laying floors so they would pass inspection of the Family Services team when they came. We didn't even have a refrigerator when we first moved back home that winter. We would store our food in the back pantry window which Dad covered with a heavy plastic on the outside. It was really cool – Dad was the king of "make-do" and was very creative about it. *We often kid about him today – he was the original "Jerry-rigger" (having the ability to improvise or retro-fit things)...we'd joke that if you look it up in a dictionary you would see Dad's picture there....and his name was Jerry V!*

We'd make a grocery list after he got home from work on Friday afternoon, and it was really a special treat to scout the cupboards with him looking for items that we needed or wanted. We were three bachelors and had a great time together ...UNTIL Dad found us a nanny. I suspect it was the Friend of the Court that demanded adult supervision, but once Betsy came on the scene – everything changed.

The first thing that she did was run me out of the kitchen – that was *her* domain. It was kind of hard going from chief cook and bottle washer to just being the oldest brat in the house (my words not hers). But, I understood that there needed to be some sense of order and adult supervision – I just didn't have to like it did I? The worst thing that happened was the drinking, arguing, and fighting that seemed to happen EVERY Friday after Dad got paid. Then they went and got groceries before heading to the bar. *(This was also a pattern we saw before Mom and Dad got divorced so many years earlier. Dad became very mean and physically violent when he drank.)*

Eventually, all six of us were back home and that was when things went from bad to worse. The arguments escalated and the fighting did too. In spite of their differences, Dad wound up marrying Betsy, and then she moved her two daughters in with us six kids. Now there were "8" kids under one roof! Don't get me wrong, we did have many good times too, but the closeness with Dad evaporated. He was either at work, out in the garage tinkering, or in the yard doing something. If he wasn't doing those things, he would sit and read the paper and you'd BETTER be quiet. Many times they would head off to the Wonder Bar for a little adult R&R.

For fun times, especially during the summer, Dad loved swimming, and if we didn't go to the mucky beach at the Bay City State Park, he would drive out to VanDerbilt Park in Tuscola County, by Quanicassee. Dad's family grew up there, and we would swim in the large inlets right off the bay. It was about the only time we got to get really close to Dad. The girls would be afraid that the water was too deep – so Dad would carry them on his back and swim across the "ditch" to the other side. We also had old rubber inner tubes that we would float on. Then we'd have a picnic back inside the park itself. For a large family of ten, it was a cheap fun-filled excursion that involved everyone.

Then it was back home again to the old routine and more rules from the kitchen. The one that stands out the most was that after baking cookies, Betsy would count them, wrap them up in a big bowl, put them in the cupboard, and they would go shopping. We were left with strict instructions to stay OUT of the cookies until she returned. Well, with eight kids and the smell of sweet cookie dough wafting through the house...somebody ate some cookies (not me). When Dad and Betsy got home, she went and counted the cookies and discovered that there was a thief in the house. Nobody confessed, so we were all called into the living room and were beaten with dad's 2 ½ inch leather belt until somebody confessed. Now that

I'm older, I understand the need for order in a house full of kids like this, but, at the time I thought it was awful – especially the punishment of the innocent.

There were some yummy things that came out of that kitchen though. I can still smell and taste the homemade banana nut bread made with fresh picked *wild* black walnuts – YUM. Dad was famous for his weekend cooking masterpieces made up of all the weekly leftovers – he proudly called it "slumgolian stew." No two weekend meals were ever the same but, believe it or not, they were all pretty tasty. The other things that we would have from time to time were fish frys. After one of the more successful fishing trips with Grandpa V, we'd all get to taste the spoils. The most unusual delicacy from these outings was the deep fried fish eggs that Dad used to make. Of course, deep fried fish eggs were an acquired taste and most of my siblings passed on eating them, but Dad and I loved them! Then there were the "Jerry's special recipes" for homemade sauerkraut, ground bologna sandwich spread with homemade dill pickles ground into the mix, and Dad's number one favorite dish – Limburger cheese with pickled bologna. Whew! I can still smell that cheese – it smelled like 6-month-old rotted gym socks! But, Dad sure loved it. Lucky for us, he also liked fresh Pinconning Sharp Cheddar cheese. We always stopped in Pinconning to visit Wilson's Cheese Shoppe whenever we went traveling north out of Bay City.

There were many - many road trips during those first couple of years they were married. We went to Lumberman's Monument, Grind Stone City, Tahquamenon Falls, Fisherman's Pier, The Mackinac Bridge, and other key landmarks all around Michigan. Adventures were part of Dad's way of unwinding and getting out of the house. It became a very important part of my life, for most of my adult life too. Later in life, we even compared our "maps" of our adventures!

My Journey In The Shadow of "The King"
........From Graceland to the Promised Land

My First Guitar

The BEST thing that came out of this new marriage was that Betsy had empathy for my passion with music and talked my dad into getting me a guitar. It was Christmas 1968 – and when I opened that gift I was in HEAVEN!

Figure 3-My first guitar
circa- 1968

After the family settled down, I immediately RAN all the way to my friend Franky's house to show it off. Franky's dad (Jose) was from Texas and played guitar and sang with a mariachi band. He agreed to show me how to play it for FREE. I carefully wrote down everything he told me on a sheet of notebook paper. I drew a picture of the guitar neck – sketched out the six strings and carefully drew horizontal lines for the little fret-bars across the strings. Then Jose would show me where to place my fingers on the strings – within the frets – and I would circle large dots on the paper to look like each chord he taught me. This was so exciting!!! I then went home and practiced and practiced and practiced some more. I had been involved in football for my first 2 years in high school – but, once I got my guitar – I quit the team. It was ALL music and entertainment for me from that point on.

Franky's family had a full color console TV (ours was a standard black and white) – and just one month earlier (November 1968) I spent most of the night there watching Elvis perform his "Comeback Special". Franky and I sang along with many of the songs! So, Jose knew of my passion to be like Elvis too. I was so impressed with the final song of the TV concert – *If I Can Dream* – it was very spiritual and uplifting. Elvis was dressed in a 2-piece white suit and to this day I can still see the veins popping out of his neck and hear his guttural raspy voice crying, "If I can stand, if I can walk, if I can think, if I can talk, if I can dream – why can't my dream - come true." All the while he was standing with his feet spread apart beyond shoulder width and swaying from side-to-side with one arm swinging like a pendulum. *WOW – how cool*, I thought. This was an Elvis move that I would incorporate into my own performances many years later....and guess what? The crowds just LOVED it!

Well, I eventually learned to play my first song on guitar - *Love Me Tender* – and was even able to sing along as I played the chords. (That's no small task for a beginner.) I was so excited when I first learned it, I ran all the way home to show my dad. Needless to say, I was pretty awkward and probably sounded off key. Dad had very little patience and shooed me out the door and told me not to bother him with that noise until I was better at playing and singing. I was crushed – but still very determined to be a singer. My fingers felt like they would bleed at times and were so tender I could hardly hold the neck of the guitar. But, I was going to get this right and I was going to be a famous singer like Elvis!!! I spent as much time as I could with Franky and his dad, Jose. I also traveled the neighborhood and sang for all the neighbors that would listen. I sang on front porches, back yards and anywhere people would allow me to show off my "new" songs.

Just a few months later, at just 15 years old, I got my first "paying" job singing for the teen club in the basement of the local YMCA on Madison Ave in Bay City, MI. I received $10 per night for singing 2 hours every other Saturday. They even put my name in the paper. Wow, I was going to be famous! The job was for me to sing in the downstairs coffee shop for about 20 minutes at a time - opposite the schedule of the main dance band playing upstairs. I was able to do this job for several weeks when I ran into my first music career challenge. Somebody "booed" me while I was singing. Wow, this was a crushing experience for a new entertainer. As I look back at it now, it was a good lesson in humility. But, at the time, it was an insult – and as the saying goes – "them are fighting words!" Fortunately, I had some good examples to follow from my time at St. Vincent's Home. The nuns taught us to bring our issues to them or the counselors and not to try and physically fight our way through these kinds of trials. So, I took a short break and I went to the manager and explained what happened. I was still quite angry about the situation, so I told him that he better get rid of the trouble-maker or I would do it myself. He had obviously had experience with this kind of issue before, because he immediately came downstairs to my microphone and announced that the room was being closed and whoever was doing the booing had better stop or not come back. Then the crowd left and went back upstairs where the main band was playing. When the band took their next break, the crowd returned to hear me sing, there were no more problems and the remainder of the night was peaceful – and fun! I was determined to get better and get more singing jobs. So I started to hang out with other musicians and singers at school. It's important to be around people that are doing or being what YOU want to become. We really do become like our friends and associates.

Life was not going really well at home and to make matters worse, Mom moved back to town and was quite upset that Dad had reclaimed the house and got all us kids back. She absolutely hated Betsy and would do whatever she could to make their life miserable. There were many arguments in front of us kids when Mom came to pick us up for visitation weekends. Of course, many of them were about how Betsy treated us – whether right or wrong – it was a major point of conflict. This too was a pattern we saw during the divorce – and now beyond. It was very stressful for all of us kids to be put in a position to choose between our parents all the time. Mom was constantly putting Dad and his new wife down. We hated the stress and at times it tore my siblings apart – because we had different opinions about many of the things Mom complained about. Of course, there were legitimate issues – but this way of handling them only caused more pain to those of us that were already going through so much! Sometimes adults don't realize how much additional suffering they cause their kids when they try to talk to them like they are adults (or their peers) – and especially when they run each other down. I have to give Dad credit, he was pretty mum when it came to discussions about our mom. He would just sigh and roll his eyes.

My Journey In The Shadow of "The King"
........From Graceland to the Promised Land

Figure 4 Pizza made with Grandma's recipe

It seemed that out of nowhere Mom rented a building on the other side of town and opened her own pizzeria. Apparently she and Grandma Josie were in it together – Grandma helped with the cooking and showed Mom and us kids how to prepare the dough and pizza sauce using an old family recipe. They called the new business Dominic's Pizzeria. (I think it was named after my mother's brother Uncle Dominic.) My brother Joe and I left Dad's house with all the turmoil and arguments and moved in with Mom so we could work in the pizzeria. Joe got pretty good at hand tossing the pizza dough in the air and spinning it. At one time we had a small audience gather and watch him prepare a "flying" pizza pie for them. It was a fabulous job. Besides making and eating all the pizza we wanted, Mom had pinball machines in the lobby and our friends would come and visit and we would hang out together for hours. Of course, I also played my guitar and sang for folks whenever I could. Things were going fairly well, and Grandma and my Uncle Dominic opened a second pizzeria in Essexville – about 15 miles from Mom's place in the south end of Bay City. Grandma and Uncle Mike worked there most of the time. I was lucky to get there once in a while to spend time with Grandma. Business was picking up, people sure loved the special sauce and excellent cheese mixture that we used.

By this time I had learned a few dozen songs on the guitar and I would play for anybody that asked me to. Mom had a friend that lived next store to her pizzeria and she would tell us to make a couple of pizzas and take them next door to feed the kids. Their Mom was also single and struggling to make ends meet. I became friends with several of the kids – and of course, I played my guitar and sang to them every time we would visit. Their Mom was an excellent piano player, and she helped me learn some of the Elvis songs that I wanted to learn. We also played many benefit concerts together – she really had a big heart for others that were less fortunate – and of course, just like me, she also just loved to sing and play music. She was an excellent ragtime piano player. She was very musically gifted – and also self-taught. She could hear a song once and immediately play it – or anything that you asked her to. Later in life, her middle son, Ricky, became a pretty good guitar player and he joined one of my bands for a while. We had a great time singing and playing together. He really had a heart for both Elvis and Gospel music – which by that time; I was playing on a regular basis too.

Then Mom began taking me and my guitar out on "advertising missions" to all the bars in town. She made me swear NOT to call her Mom in public – I was her little brother when there were other people around. We had a lot of great adventures around all those bars in Bay City (It has the dubious honor of having the most bars per capita in Michigan). I was shocked the first time a guy at a bar offered me $5 to sing *Love Me Tender* to his girlfriend. I was just 16, and in 1969, $5.00 was a lot of money to a teenager. (According to dollartimes.com that is worth nearly $35.00 today!) You could still buy a 16 ounce glass bottle of Pepsi and a Banana Flip for 25 cents! As a teenager, I was one of only a very few teenage kids that went out on a Saturday night and actually came home with more money than I left with. What special memories these were for me and Mom. She was sure the life of the party – and she seemed right at home in all those bars.

In 1969, Mom had an old Ford convertible. It was a pretty beat up and rusty thing so she let my brother Joe and I paint it. We went to Larson's Salvage and bought about five cans of spray paint – all wild psychedelic colors. When we got done with that car, it looked like somebody had eaten a huge pizza with EVERYTHING (including anchovies) and barfed all over the poor car. It was really something else.....but, to us it was a hippie's piece of art! I don't know what ever happened to that car, but we sure got some funny looks from people when we came driving down the conservative streets of downtown Bay City.

Then, the pizzeria closed and things started to get rough at Mom's house. There were parties, boyfriends and late nights; it was hard to find peace and quiet for doing school work or hardly anything else. It was also not the healthiest atmosphere for teens to grow up in, so I set up another meeting with the case worker and moved back in with Dad and Betsy.

My Journey In The Shadow of "The King"
........From Graceland to the Promised Land

All through high school I spent most of my spare time in music, choir, drama classes and plays, with other musicians, entertainers and singers. It was around this time that Elvis was awarded his first Grammy for "How Great Thou Art" - so I learned how to play it on my guitar. From the first time I sang it, people's reaction was so great, and I felt so moved myself, I made it a permanent part of my act from that day forward. I loved to sing it. What amazing words and dedication to our God. I also learned Amazing Grace – and sang that as often as I could too. I would wake up an hour or two early every day before school and lie on the living room floor with headphones on and listen to Elvis music. It was really nice, because I could hear the details of his breathing, inflections, phrasing and guttural style of singing – and still do it without bothering anybody in the house. I had a burning desire to be a singer like Elvis – and that was my main focus in life. I studied and imitated him in every way I could. Along the way, I also remembered God – and stayed true to my Catechism lessons. I did not stray from the Ten Commandments. I was not a girl chaser – nor a drug sampler. During my teen years, I was often teased by my friends about being a "goody-goody". I didn't cuss like many of my friends did and many of my peers would make snide remarks about my sideburns and call me "Elvis-the-pelvis". I just let it roll off – I was actually proud to be recognized for my Elvis-like persona. This heckling was a little painful at the time, but I learned later in life to be able to withstand even more stress over my religious views and the way I chose to worship God.

During this time, my family was pretty poor, so I worked in the high school kitchen in exchange for a hot lunch. I always brought my guitar in and would sing for the kitchen help whenever I got the chance. Then I'd sit on the cafeteria tables and sing to anybody that would stop by and listen to me. I just LOVED singing – and would do it whenever I got the chance. I became friends with Biff Williams – who sang like Hank Williams (I don't think they were related) – and we sang some Elvis and Hank songs together for quite a long time. I remember going over to Biff's house and listening to Hank – and Biff would listen to Elvis – then we'd try to do some new songs of each one. My favorite Hank Williams song was *I'm So Lonesome I Could Cry*. It was years later that I discovered Elvis recorded a version of it too! I also liked

Cold, Cold Heart and *Your Cheatin' Heart*. I would "Elvis-ize" Cheatin' Heart – and Biff and his dad would just roll their eyes and laugh. I'd modulate the last verse up one step – and get real guttural – and drag out–"when-tears-come-a-doooowwwwwnnnnnnn – Like-ah-fallllllllin'-rraaaiiiinn....you'll-ah-toss-ahhh-rooouund...and-a-call-ahhh-my-name!!!!" It was a blast – I loved watching the expressions on their faces as I experimented with the Elvis sounds on non-Elvis songs.

Another musical friend, Jim Sample played guitar like Chet Atkins – Jim taught me quite a bit about guitar too. If I remember correctly, it was Jim that helped me learn the Elvis top ten hit song, *All Shook Up*. I can still see my mom's eyes get real big when I played it for her the first time. She was so excited! "You're gonna make a million dollars and buy your momma a house!" she used to say. I still hung out with Franky and his dad, Jose, and also Franky's Cousin Juan whenever I could. Wherever there was live music going on, I did everything in my power to be there. I went to school dances, radio station events and anything that was happening musically in and around the area. I even made it out to a couple "Battle of the Bands" events. (Even though I was underage and usually had walk or ride my bike for miles to get there.)

I tried out for several new teenage "rock" bands and sang with some of them a few times. They would let me go after a few practices because they said I sounded too much like "Elvis" and they were doing "modern" 60's rock music – like the Doors, Santana, the Beatles and others. I changed directions and became friends with many local country singers and became a member of some of those types of bands. I performed with some popular local entertainers like Max and Dale Cueller, Butch Heath and Bill Pelton. Bill formed a country band called "The Michigan Playboys" and we played around the area for several months. Later I connected with a famous country DJ named Dusty Rhodes from WXOX radio out of Saginaw. He and I had a 2-piece band (he played drums) and we played in Midland, MI at a club called the Silver Dollar. It was all a LOT of fun and we really had some great adventures. In order to be discovered and get "famous", I attended many-many talent shows. I never won any of them though, they were usually won by little kids or some duet or other (family related) talent that the judges knew. At first I was a little jealous of the winners. I guess I ultimately learned that being an imitator was NOT the best talent to have for these kinds of contests. It also left a bad taste in my spirit about using music to compete with others. I loved to sing for the sake of singing (and also praising God) – I didn't need to prove to anybody that I was the best, or needed to be the first-place singer. Those kinds of motives seemed ugly to me – because you ultimately had to wish others would fail so you could be the winner.

On a positive note, the exposure from being involved in those contests wound up paying off for me. I wound up making a lot of new friends (and fans) and through a mutual friend named Char, I met Bob and Kaye Coats from Pretty-Coat Productions. They booked me as an opening act for country music greats like Ferlin Husky, Tex Ritter, Jack Blanhcard & Misty Morgan, Tommy Cash, Stella Parton and many more. It was 1969-1970 and I was only 16-17 years old when all this happened in Bay City. Musically, it was really looking good for reaching my goal of getting my own Graceland someday!

I played multiple shows for Pretty-Coat Productions all around the state. I even got to drive Ferlin Husky from Bay City to Ludington in my car. It was really a special trip for me. We talked for nearly the whole trip. He told me he had a son that died and would have been my age and was thrilled to be able to sing with me and travel between shows with me. It gave him a sense of what it might have been like with his own son. Not only did I get pictures with him, but when we parted company in Ludington, Michigan, he gave me one of his little brown cigarettes with his name printed on it, he smoked these when off stage.

I also got to meet and talk with Tex Ritter – that "Gringo with the Lilacs all covered with dew"....and I asked him what advice he would give a young singer who wanted to make it big in music. He smoked one of those Sherlock Holmes-style pipes – you know the one that curls down. As he pondered his answer, he puffed a little smoke, crossed his arms and looked down at me and said, "Son, music is a business. "You have to treat it like one if you want to be successful." What a true statement – I saw lots of local musicians and singers just act like they were always on the amateur talent show stage. They'd show up late, sing or play off-key due to drinking. Even worse, they'd do more songs than they were allowed and make the management and all the other talent upset because they ran over their allotted time. Anyway, I took Tex's words to heart and was always very serious and professional in the way I conducted myself around my music and the gigs I worked. These were some excellent opportunities for me and I learned a lot about the music business from the pros during my early years.

My Journey In The Shadow of "The King"
........From Graceland to the Promised Land

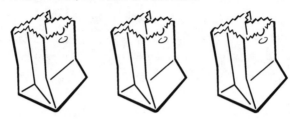

One weekend in the early summer of 1970, my dad and step-mom planned to go camping with the whole family. Well, as an older teen, I really didn't want to go – especially since there was a big WXOX radio-sponsored talent show that weekend. Luckily, I had a co-op job through school working at Burger King and I was scheduled to work that Friday night. So, I was allowed to stay home alone as long as I behaved myself. On Saturday afternoon I went to the talent show and when I came off the stage a man approached me. He had a daughter there who was also singing in the show. He explained that he was from Cadillac and his wife was a HUGE Elvis fan. He asked if I would sing for her over the phone. Of course, not knowing who they might be - or if they might even know Johnny Carson – I quickly agreed. ...And, it didn't hurt that his 16-year-old daughter sang like Tammy Wynette and was pretty good looking too.

We hung out together for the rest of the show and got to know each other fairly well during that time. At the end of the afternoon, when the talent show was over, Earl asked me what I was doing for the rest of the weekend. When I said I had nothing planned, he invited me to come up to Cadillac with him and his daughter so I could meet his wife and sing for her. It sounded like more fun than I had planned for myself, so I grabbed my guitar and we headed out for a little adventure. As I look back on it, I didn't know this guy from Adam, and he certainly could have had many ulterior motives in talking me into coming home with him and his daughter. God was truly in all of this – and I sensed it was a good thing to do.

It was a long drive from Saginaw to Cadillac and I was pretty wired from all the singing and radio personalities at the talent show. We talked and talked during the drive – and I spilled my guts out about my dreams of being a famous singer someday. His daughter had similar dreams – that's why they drove all the way from Cadillac to be in the show. As I told them about what was happening in my life, Earl's wheels were clicking and churning. When we got to Cadillac, his whole family treated me like I was "The King." I got preferential treatment on everything. Then they showed me around the town and told me about the local teen nightclub called The Platters just outside of town. Earl explained that many Detroit and other national acts came there to sing – and that he thought I was good enough to be on that stage with them. He also said his daughter should be there too. He asked if I could learn some of her songs so we could sing together – of course, I said YES!

That night the family offered to take me in and get me out of all the craziness I was experiencing at "both homes" back in Bay City. School was out and I needed an opportunity to be "discovered" – so I said yes. The next day Earl drove me back to Bay City and I packed everything I owned into three paper grocery bags and left home at age of 17. I wrote a note to my dad that said: "You've done enough, I'll take it from here." I taped it on the phone on the wall that had been ripped down so many times when I was younger. On the note, I gave them the phone number of where I was now "living" in Cadillac.

Dad was NOT impressed with my brief goodbye note. He called the house in Cadillac on Sunday evening when they got home and said, "Daniel, get your ass home right now. I'll come up there and get you if I have to."

I told him that I was now an emancipated minor – living with a tax-paying family and that I could leave home if I wanted to. I assured him I was okay and that I would finish high school. I just didn't want to live like I was living anymore – and these nice people agreed to take me in. I guess that argument did the trick. He stopped calling and I was now on my own. It was both an exciting and somewhat scary feeling. But, once again, I felt this was the BEST thing for me, as my high school counselor back in Bay City had tried to help me see during one of our earlier sessions.

Life with my new family was really a lot of fun at first. We did a lot of things together – shopping, movies, and driving adventures around the hills of the Cadillac area. Cadillac was considered *Up North* to people where I was born and raised. It was about 95 miles (an hour and a half drive) northwest of Bay City. There were miles and miles of wooded forests covering some beautiful rolling hills. In fact, there was also a mountain of sorts and a famous ski lodge there called Caberfae – it's still in operation today! During the summer it is a golf resort.

One of the most unique aspects of Cadillac is the channel that connects the two major lakes – Lake Mitchell and Lake Cadillac. When winter sets in, the channel immediately freezes over until the lakes freeze. Then the channel opens up and no matter how cold it gets outside, the channel never freezes over again! It is said to be one of the most unusual wonders of the world. I have to tell you that it gets pretty cold in Cadillac – I remember walking across Lake Mitchell to get to school in the dead of winter and I personally saw the open water in the channel when it was 3-4 degrees below zero outside. It was an awesome site.

I wasn't satisfied with just living there with my new family; I had to do something to contribute my share to the household (something both Mom and Dad taught me). So, I got a job at the local Dairy Freeze ice cream parlor. It was a decent paying job for a 17 year old and I liked the perks – free ice cream sundaes. My favorite became a strawberry sundae with hot fudge, nuts and whipped cream on it. YUM! I got to be a pretty good short order cook too. Besides that, I also took singing jobs wherever I could – but, they were few and far between for teenagers in a small resort town. By this time I had lost contact with my entertainment friends from Bay City, so I wasn't getting any more of those bookings. Years later I learned that they were shocked when I all but disappeared so quickly.

My Journey In The Shadow of "The King"
........From Graceland to the Promised Land

As the summer went on, I noticed that Earl was pretty generous with his daughter. I mean he would take the rest of the family, two boys and another younger daughter and his wife on one or two excursions per week and leave me and Tammy alone. Sometimes he would even give us the keys to the station wagon and send the two of us off to the drive-in movies alone. I mean, come on folks, two hormone-driven teenagers all alone for hours at a time...what's a guy to do? Even though I was a goody-goody and more Godly than most of my friends – I was still a teenage human male!!! I thank God we never got into the serious kind of trouble that I later figured her daddy was hoping for. I discovered that Earl was on SSI disability due to several heart attacks and that he was planning on cashing in on the new Elvis and Tammy duet that he expected me to put together. I also learned that Tammy had a boyfriend and was going steady when I showed up – and that she immediately dumped her boyfriend the day after I arrived in town. Her older brother let me in on a lot of these family secrets.

The other thing that happened toward the end of summer was that Earl began really coming down on me about learning the new duet music. I wasn't learning it fast enough for him. The problem was that I was a fairly *new* guitar player and so it took me quite a while to even learn how to play my new Elvis songs which I already knew how to sing from all those early-morning living room headset sessions. I wasn't familiar with Tammy's country songs at all, and singing duet harmony was a completely new experience for me. It seemed like I went from King to skunk in the house when Earl was around. He even called me out one day when I got home from work with my paycheck and several bags of groceries. He scowled at me and said,

"Who do you think you are? I took you in and rescued you from all that violence. Now you go walking around my house like you own it – with your nose stuck up in the air."

Man - was he ever mad. I guess my groceries must have stepped on a nerve. I started seeing that there was obviously something wrong with this picture.

My Journey In The Shadow of *"The King"*
........*From Graceland to the Promised Land*

Well as I began to figure all these things out school was starting back up and Tammy and I had a new set of challenges – her old boyfriend! He hated my guts and had a little gang that was out to get me. It seems we were bound to meet up at some point and – sure enough - one day after lunch he and his buddies cornered me. I tried to explain to him that I didn't even know he existed until weeks after I arrived in town, but he didn't care. All he knew was that I took his girl and he was going to kick my butt for it. So he attacked me right then and there on school property.

All of my life I was never a "fighter", I always tried to reason things out, but, he just came running right at me. I was able to knock him down and get him into a scissors hold – where I squeezed his abdomen and back between my legs. It's an old wrestling move that Leaping Larry Shane, a wrestler from the 1960's, was famous for. Even though I refused to fight with him – and let him up a couple of times – he repeatedly attacked me and it was ticking me off. I finally just knocked him down again and continued to squeeze him in the scissors hold over and over again until he nearly passed out. They told me he was even coughing up blood.

By this time one of the teachers came and broke up the "fight." I remember the principle was pretty upset about the whole episode, but he calmed down when he discovered that I was protecting myself in self-defense. He also commented that when he looked up my records, he was impressed that I had such good grades. He advised me to steer clear of these trouble-makers. I happily did just that.

Ultimately, I learned that the main reason I was brought to town was to be used by Tammy's dad to make money for the family. This was quite a depressing discovery for me. How could somebody go to such lengths to use another person like that – and even leverage his own daughter as bait? It was actually a little scary to me. If he was willing to do all that, what else was he capable of? There was no other option in my mind; I had to get clear of this whole mess. So, I broke off the relationship with Tammy and moved out of the family's house and into the house of my Dairy Freeze boss.

My Journey In The Shadow of "The King"
........From Graceland to the Promised Land

At the time, I thought this was a very lucky move. Of course, I was still just a naïve high-school teenager. I began noticing that my boss spent a lot of time with his assistant manager, Rob, off hours. One night they stayed up real late. I discovered that Rob's car was still there in the morning when I went to school. I really didn't think too much of it at the time. A few weeks into my stay, I was struggling with my breakup with Tammy and all the things that went on with her family as I was leaving the situation (it wasn't a happy breakup). After all the struggles in my own family, the deceitfulness I just experienced was a major let-down for me. All I wanted in life was some peace and a loving home life. I was pretty upset about being let down by another set of selfish adults.

Well, I got my hands on some cigarettes and beer. I didn't really smoke or drink at the time, but I was very depressed over all these changes. Then, I drank 4-or-5 beers and got drunk and very dizzy from smoking cigarettes and I guess during the night I vomited all over the cot and blankets that my boss had provided me to sleep on. He was very angry about the mess (he had to clean it up during the night – I didn't even know it happened) and then he told me I had to go; he could not put up with these kinds of episodes in his house. I discovered later that I was also apparently cramping his lifestyle.

The next day I moved into a local hotel that offered discounts for weekly rates. I have to confess, this was the first time in my life that I was totally alone! I dreaded coming home from school each day – there was nothing and no one in my one-room apartment. The hotel was located in a dreary old building in downtown Cadillac. It was the off-season and things were unusually quiet – something quite unique to me since I grew up in a home with five siblings. Tammy's family was large and noisy too! I was used to constant interaction and companionship. The emptiness of the hotel room echoed through my body and I was very lonely and depressed. The year was 1970 and there were no cell phones, internet or cable and I had no TV and very little money. On top of that, I was a minor. There really was nothing to do all night long, especially on school nights. At times I wasn't sure how long I could take the biting loneliness.

I ultimately signed up for a co-op job through school and started working for Montgomery Wards and quit my job at Dairy Freeze. Things were looking up for a while – then one day I was unexpectedly called into the principal's office. Apparently, somebody notified his office that I was no longer living with Tammy's family and as a 17-year-old minor, I was not entitled to go to school unless I had a guardian and was living with a tax-paying family of some sort. I was devastated. What was I going to do? I wanted to finish high school and get my diploma. Going back to Bay City was NOT an option! The principal was very sympathetic of my problem. He said he was impressed with my grades and my behavior and he would do whatever he could do to help me.

We made a plan during that little meeting. I would contact the Department of Social Services and see if they could find me a foster home and he would mention my situation to his staff to see if any of them knew anybody who would be willing to take me in for the remainder of the school year.

My Journey In The Shadow of "The King"
........From Graceland to the Promised Land

Well wouldn't you know it, God came through again. There was an English teacher at Cadillac High School (CHS) that stepped forward. She and her husband agreed to give me a 30-day trial stay at their house. It turned out that Mr. Stanley was a Protestant Minister – so once again I was surrounded by Godly people. It was just incredible how all this fell into place. Of course, I embraced my new family and the multiple church services that they conducted per week. The Stanleys - Dirk and Sherry - were impressed with my dedication to both school and domestic chores (although Sherry did most of them) and that I also had a Godly attitude. So, I had a NEW home – much nicer and far more stable than the two I had just escaped from. My mood improved, I found peace at last.

Having a *parent* as a teacher in my school was quite a different experience for me. Luckily, I was not assigned to any of Sherry's classes. But something really good came from this relationship – ENCOURAGEMENT! Although Dirk and Sherry had mixed feelings about me hanging out at the Platters Teen Club on weekends, they encouraged me to get involved in as many school activities as I wanted. I was already in the Choir and Music Theory classes, but, Sherry also signed me up for the school play and National Honor Society. I was accepted into both. In fact, I wound up with the leading role in the High School play that year – it was called "Bull in a China Shop." What a tremendously fun time that was – even if it wasn't a musical.

As an Elvis impersonator/singer, I was already good at memorizing words to songs. Adapting that to lines in a play was a fairly easy stretch for me. Then acting out the stage direction was also of little effort, because I wasn't alone on the stage like when I was out front singing all by myself. In the play I was interacting with others – and I seemed to take to it like a fly on honey. It really was SWEET!

Back at my new home, I spent so much time in my room memorizing all my words and actions that I was way ahead of the rest of the cast in learning my lines – so, I started helping others and showing them how to memorize their lines (which also helped me in the end because I could anticipate all of the activity on the stage). I guess I didn't realize how much I was helping the other cast members – because I was having so much FUN with it. Then at the end of rehearsals we started practicing the curtain call. The curtain call is where when the play ends, they draw the final curtain and then all the actors come out one at a time and take a bow. Well, I was watching everybody get called out but me – and I was getting worried – I walked over to one of my friends who was one of the widows in the play and expressed my concern and she said to me – with a surprised look on her face,
"Danny, you have the leading role, you come out last!"
That was the first time that I realized the position I was playing in the play.

Of course, during the multiple weeks we spent together, even though this was not a musical play, I brought my guitar in and sang for anyone that would listen. We just had a blast with every aspect of the play. The overall story of *Bull in a China Shop* was focused around an apartment full of four spinsters who were madly in love with a bachelor police detective living across the street from them. The play opens with them fighting over who should have the binoculars next while they spied on Detective Dennis O'Finn inside of his apartment. Unfortunately Mr. O'Finn is a homicide detective, so the ladies hatch a plot to kill off one of their own in order to bring Mr. O'Finn into their home. When they succeed, not only does Mr. O'Finn show up, but there is also a foxy female reporter that arrives and has designs on the detective herself. It is just a hoot to see all of the comical situations that arose. Anyway, as a bachelor myself at the time, and singing like Elvis, there were some similarities going on in real life as we acted out the play. I never really got serious about any of my co-stars (like Elvis did) but, we dated a few times and had several cast parties and birthday parties during the run of the play. It was a great opportunity for me to meet people, especially since this was my first year at the school. I was grateful to Sherry for her wise guidance and encouragement.

Figure 5 Cadillac High School 1971 - Singing for the whole school assembly

In the meantime, I continued to sing in choir and wrote a song in music theory class that was selected to be performed for the whole school assembly just before graduation.

Over that past year or so, when I was doing a lot of singing and practicing, I experienced several laryngitis episodes where I completely lost my voice. When I shared this with my choir teacher, he suggested I get some vocal lessons and gave me the name of a woman in town that he said was an expert vocal coach. So, I called her up and scheduled myself for vocal lessons. She told me to bring my guitar for the first lesson. When I got there we sat down and talked a little about my background and my future goals. Then she asked me to sing her a couple songs. I sang *Love Me Tender* and then started screaming out my version of *Jailhouse Rock*. That's when she stopped me and we spent the remainder of the hour practicing my breathing. She pointed out that I was singing and straining to hit notes from my throat. This was a common mistake most people make in order to get a sound they are trying to achieve. She had me sing the musical scale (do-ra-mi-fa-so-la-ti-do) as if I was Santa Claus Ho-Ho-Ho-ing. Then she said to feel the air come through my diaphragm as I sang – and to take deeper breaths before any loud or long sections of the song.

So, off I went – Ho-Ho-Ho-ing all the way home. I practiced over and over all week long and even tried to apply this new style to my guitar playing songs – and....IT WORKED!!! It was a huge help and I could actually feel the difference (although my stomach and chest were getting tired from all the extra singing). When I returned for my second lesson the following week, she had me sing the scales and then listened to a couple of songs. After that she reminded me of the mechanics of singing from my diaphragm – and finally, she sat me down and said the following...

"Danny, you are what we call a natural in the business. Listen to me carefully – you can sing like nobody I've heard before at your age. Take what I've taught you and practice it until it becomes second nature to you. Then – forget about vocal teachers – we will kill what you already have. Don't EVER go to another lesson again!"

And with that, she refused to take my money – thanked me for singing to her and sent me on my way. Wow – what a strange vocal teacher I thought. But, when I shared this with my choir teacher back at school, he said he wasn't surprised.

As the days went along, there were some tense moments during the remainder of the school year – some at school – like when Tammy made a scene in the choir room shortly after our breakup. She ultimately quit the choir and joined another group instead. There was also a midnight-hour problem that cropped up when my step-mom, Betsy, called the Stanley's house several days in a row between midnight and 3am because she and my dad were having fights again.

She would call crying and tell me that Dad hit her. One time he broke her jaw and she had to have it wired shut for several weeks. I finally had to tell her to stop calling me. (What did she expect a 17-year-old to do from 95 miles away?) Sherry warned me that if the calls didn't stop, they would have to find me another place to live. I pleaded with Betsy to either leave my dad – or get some other help. But, she had to STOP calling me at those late hours. Luckily, the calls stopped and I was able to stay in my new home.

One of the hardest aspects of living in Cadillac was the guilt I felt for abandoning my brothers and sisters. I had been raised to look after them and watch over them all my life. Leaving them like I did was a shock to them and me both. To make up for it, I wrote letters to them telling them about my adventures. My sister Janet kept her letters and showed them to me many years later. She said they were very encouraging to her and everybody else. It was many years later that others heard parts of this story and also encouraged me to write this book in order to encourage other people living through similar circumstances.

During those troubling years back in Bay City, I had spent many hours in a room with my high school counselor, Mrs. Ruby. She taught me to think things through: what were the symptoms? What did I want the outcome to be? Who were some mature adults that I respected and could trust to guide me to the proper solution? She said it was always best to get several opinions before I acted on anything important. I later learned there was a Bible verse for this – Proverbs 15:22 – *"there is wisdom in a multitude of counsel."* I have used this method of creating a guiding circle around myself for many years. At one time, I over-used it by confiding in too many people. Some of them the wound up being the wrong people.....I'll get into that as we migrate through the years.

While I was in Cadillac, I depended mostly on Dirk and Sherry and the Drama teacher, Mrs. U, to help advise me when I got confused about life issues or family matters. Dirk and Sherry helped me see that I needed to distance myself from my broken-family activities because I had taken on too much responsibility and I needed to be a kid myself. As hard as it was to separate myself from my family, I knew they were right, and I needed to get on with my life.

My primary goal for my life continued to be music and God, I spent a lot of time in choir and the music room as well as attending concerts at the Platters where I met many touring bands. One of the bands was from Detroit and they invited me to come down and sit in with them. I would hitch-hike on weekends from Cadillac to Detroit to sing with the band at a teen club called "Cupid's Den" located at 14 mile and John R. My job at Montgomery Ward's helped me support my music goals.

My Journey In The Shadow of "The King"
........From Graceland to the Promised Land

Since I went to Cupid's Den and was a "guest singer" so often, I became friends with the owner, Gene, and wound up staying at his house for some of the weekends I visited. Before that, I would crash with the bands at someone's house – or party pad. I was not very comfortable with the band arrangement because there was a lot of sex and drugs at those after hour's events. I was quite fortunate that there were never any busts or arrests when I was there. I think Gene saw that I was different in that respect and took me in to help shelter me from all that stuff. (Now I know for sure that God had a hand in all of this too.)

The Stanley's continued to encourage my artistic abilities and my goals. They even co-signed for the loan for my first car. God seemed to always be watching out for me – I could have wound up dropping out of high school if this couple had not come along to take me in. Of course, like I did earlier in my life at the St. Vincent's Home/Orphanage, I took an interest in my surroundings and went to church several times a week with the preacher and his wife. Since he was a preacher, we also spent a lot of time socializing with many prominent people of the community. I was able to sing for some of them and became friends with their teenage kids. I still have contact with a couple of them today. I continue to be grateful to God for the many "good" people He brought into my life.

The Golden Rule

When I graduated from CHS, one of the supervisors at Montgomery Wards gave me a graduation and going-away gift. She said that it represented what she saw of my lifestyle – It was a plaque of the Golden Rule.

What an awesome challenge to give to an impressionable 18-year-old

---

The Golden Rule...

I REALIZED YEARS LATER THAT IT
WAS JESUS THAT SPOKE THOSE
WORDS IN Matthew 7:12.

---

graduate – **"Do unto others as you would have them do unto you."**
Whether she really saw that in me or not, just by declaring it over my life
and giving me that plaque, made me feel like I had to measure up to
that for the rest of my life. I still get teary-eyed when I think about it. It
was just beautiful. I hung it up in my home office for many years – until it
fell and broke. But, I can still see it in my mind's eye – a tan plaque with
some of the most powerful words presented to me as a young adult.

My Journey In The Shadow of "The King"
........From Graceland to the Promised Land

n June 1971 I graduated with honors and was a member of the National Honor Society. I was offered a college scholarship, but declined because I wanted to be a famous singer someday and ultimately get my own "Graceland" like Elvis did for his family. So, I arranged to transfer my job with Montgomery Wards from Cadillac to the Wonderland Mall in Livonia (just outside Detroit) in order to be "discovered."

I searched the Detroit newspapers and found an ad where I could pay room and board at a home with an elderly couple near the mall where the store was located. Unfortunately, within a few weeks, I discovered this couple also had severe marital problems and I knew that I needed to move out. I also realized during that time that working at Ward's was NOT the lifestyle I wanted to live

It wasn't long before I met Jim Kowalew. Jim was selling Kirby Vacuum cleaners for Jeff Franklin and I applied for a job as a salesman. Of course, I sang for everybody that asked – and Jim was curious about my ability. We immediately hit it off and were quickly best friends!

One of my best memories with Jim was when we would drive to a quiet neighborhood and park my car, set up a Kirby Vacuum Cleaner display kit on the hood – and then I would start playing my guitar to draw a crowd. While I was singing, Jim would promote the Kirby. We also did something similar for Jeff at the local Flea market where he had a booth. What a racket that guy had – he would hire high school grads and teach us the basics on selling. Then, before we left every client's house, he would insist on having us call the office and talk to him. If the people were on the fence about the sale, he would trade over the phone with them – ANYTHING of value that he could sell at the flea market would be fair game to reduce the price of the Kirby. It was a real circus act!!!

I lost my confidence in Jeff when he came into the morning sales meeting one day and was bragging about selling a deluxe Kirby system to a couple that lived in a shack with a dirt floor! YES – he demanded it was true – and we believed him. They had a dirt floor, but they realized they needed a clean bed and the Kirby cleaned a mattress like nothing else on the market. Man, he was a character.

Jim had a friend named Tim K. who was a well-known entertainer and had a booking agent that was always looking for talent. Tim introduced me to Al Cole – and Al began booking me immediately at Moose Lodges and Elks clubs all around Michigan. I was amazed at my first payday after I began working with Al Cole – it was for performing at the Saginaw Moose Lodge. I was told to show up early and be the second act that night by following a 20-minute show by an exotic dancer. I had never seen an exotic dancer before

Figure 6 Saginaw Moose "Floor Show" 1974

and this was a bit of an eye opener for me. I got dressed when she went on stage and when she finished her "dancing" (more like stripping) I came out and sang 20 minutes of Elvis songs while sitting on a bar stool with my electric guitar (the one that Betsy gave me). At the end of the night they called me over to the bar and paid me $45. I told the nightclub manager that there must have been a mistake, $45 was too much money for just 5 songs (this was from an 18-year-old in 1971 – it would be worth $278 in 2018) – Bob Blake just laughed and said – "NO, this is correct, you get ALL this money."

You have to remember that 1971 was before the oil embargo and the spike in gas prices. At that time in Detroit there were gas wars going on – I could literally fill up my 1977 Pontiac Catalina for less than $2.00 (gas was under .15-cents a gallon back then!) So $45 was a HUGE amount of money to me! With paydays like this, I knew entertaining was exactly where I wanted to be. All that FUN, applause from the audience, good looking exotic dancers and big paydays – WOW!

While I was selling Kirby Vacuum cleaners, I became friends with another young salesman named Randy, who still lived at home. Randy talked his parents into letting me live with them a while so I could get out of the bad marriage couple's room and board situation. Well it seems marriage problems were all around me back then. While I was staying at Randy's I had a little crush on his younger sister (but, she was really a little young for me). So every chance I got, I would try to spend time at the house so I could be around her.

One afternoon, in between sales appointments, I went back to the house and was outside talking to Randy's sister when his dad's car screeched around the corner and slammed to a halt in front of the house. His dad jumped out and headed right for me – grabbed me by my neck and picked me up and carried me into the house. I had NO idea what was going on. He was mumbling something about sneaking around with her...I thought he meant his daughter...until he carried me by the neck into his bedroom and shoved my face into the mattress! Then he started yelling about me having sex with his wife!

"Right here where you two did it"
"Whoa!" I said, "I have never had sex with your wife. I wouldn't do that. It was your daughter I was after."

I didn't realize what I was saying with all the adrenaline pumping through my body. By this time his wife had come in and was trying to calm him down. She denied the claims too. Then Randy showed up out of nowhere and started pulling his dad off me (I was getting faint from lack of oxygen). When Randy and his Mom finally calmed his dad down – I jumped up and ran for my car. I got the heck out of there! I had to start looking for a new place to live.

My Journey In The Shadow of "The King"
........From Graceland to the Promised Land

Randy met me back at the office and brought my clothes and stuff. (Luckily my guitar was ALWAYS with me in my car.) We both agreed that I should never come around his house again.

So, my new best friend Jim Kowalew talked to his friend Tim K again and set up a brief interview with me and Tim so we could talk about the potential for me to stay at his apartment. It didn't even phase me that Tim met me at the door precisely at the agreed upon time all wet and wrapped in a towel. As he opened his apartment door with a smile, he said that he just got out of the shower. I should have gotten suspicious when he just stayed in the towel and sat on the living room couch during the 45 minute interview. We talked about my job and what kind of lifestyle Tim had as an evening nightclub entertainer. I was okay with all of it, so, I moved in with Tim K the next day.

Things with Tim went along pretty well and since he was a formally trained piano player, (at Julliard I believe) I was looking forward to learning some new things about music from him. Although, he appeared to have little patience with me at times – because I was just a kid (he was at least 10-15 years older than me). I think he saw my self-taught guitar playing as a little crude compared to his refined piano playing.

Jim and I would frequently visit Tim at the classy Georgian Inn where Tim had a well-paying steady gig. He even got paid vacations there. We also traveled along with Tim when he made other guest appearances with other entertainers – like Judy Deary and Edna Brown. In the meantime, I was also continuing to entertain for Al Cole at many different Moose, Elks and Eagles clubs around Detroit, Saginaw, Lansing and other places. I was meeting some very well-known professional comedians and other performers while playing at these clubs – which we affectionately called the "Animal Circuit".

Once again things were looking up and seemed to be going along quite well for me. Until...one night, several weeks later, Tim hosted an after-hours guys-only party, and one of his drunken visitors attempted to molest me while I was sleeping. Tim stopped the man when he heard me scream,

"What the Hell are you doing?"

I was so upset by the whole episode that I moved out the next day. I stayed with Jim and his dad for a few days while I looked for another permanent place to stay. When I look back at the situation, I see the hand of God guarding me against multiple potential attacks. For some reason I had been placed in situations that could have been devastating if any of these men decided to take advantage of me – either in my sleep or by overpowering me – or even by drugging me. But, by the Grace of God, I was able to live through them with healthy memories of how God protected me from any such negative outcomes.

By this time I was running out of options on where to live. I knew I didn't want to stay at a hotel or try to rent an apartment on my own. (I was too young, didn't have any credit yet, and this city was not as teenager friendly as Cadillac was.) So, knowing that I had many Italian relatives in the Detroit area, I called my mom and asked her for a few names and numbers. Of course, she asked me to move back to Bay City – which I was not interested in doing at all. She finally gave me a couple names and numbers of our distant relatives in the Detroit area and I made some phone calls.

I wound up staying with one of my distant cousins - Marie and her husband Rob.

They talked me into getting a factory-type job where Rob worked. When I moved in with them, I wasn't making steady money selling Kirby's since I lost my enthusiasm after being kicked out of several houses due to Jeff's strong-arm sales tactics. Then, I completely lost my confidence in the vacuum sales business when I discovered how much middleman markup there was and how much Jeff was making off of each sale. It was refreshing to get into a steady income job, and Rob even drove us to work most of the time – at least at the beginning of our relationship.

Within a month or so, Rob began working some very long hours and I decided to drive separately because I needed to leave on weekends before he was ready to go home. I was still doing some singing and had several dates with Jim and others to try and get more entertainment bookings. We continued to visit Tim and other entertainers as well as cruising Gratiot Avenue on weekends. I was definitely a teenager – and I was having my fun while I still could!

As the summer progressed, my buddy Franky (whose dad trained me on guitar) came down from Bay City and wanted to get involved in Detroit area entertainment too. So I helped him get a job at the Kirby sales office and I arranged to have him stay with one of my other cousins. That was an eye-opening experience for my cousin, and me as well. I learned things about Franky that I never knew before. He was a very self-centered young fellow and caused quite a scene over at Cousin Lacey's house. She called me and Marie several times complaining about some of the things he had done.

I had to quit the daytime job after they nearly worked me to death over the summer (6 -7 days and 50-60-hours per week). Hey, I was going to be an entertainer – not a factory rat! With all my late-night escapades and cruising the strips, I was ultimately asked to move out of my cousin's house because of all the coming and going at all hours of the days and nights (and they had small children at home). About the same time, Cousin Lacey finally ran Franky out of her house too.

It just so happened that while I was performing at some different social events throughout Detroit, I met a man that was forming a special "Show Band" up in Saginaw and so Franky and I agreed to join the band and we moved into an apartment together up in Saginaw. We also shared the opportunity with Franky's cousin, Juan who was a phenomenal guitar player. Together with a great keyboard player named Rick, we created a top-class show band that was VERY successful. We called ourselves "The Variations" because we were composed of two Italians and two Mexicans.

Shortly after we started playing together, the band manager came up to me with tickets to an Elvis concert in Detroit at the Olympia Theater in 1972. We were in the nose bleed section – and luckily he brought a couple pairs of binoculars. I was just mesmerized when Elvis hit the stage. First, the music started – the crowd began to stir – the electricity in the place swelled and then "R-O-A-R!" - The crowd went nuts! Elvis was jumping around like a Mexican Jumping Bean on a HOT PLATE! I saw incredible things that night. It was hard to hear the singing, but, I sure learned a lot about his dancing. What a terrific night that was. I read everything I could get my hands on about Elvis. Most things were from magazines, but the story that I remembered the most was about how he experimented with his own dancing style. He said he would wiggle his leg and the girls went wild. His manager told him to go out and do it again. Then Elvis would try different things and if they got a good response, he would keep doing them. If not, he would drop them.

So I did the same basic thing – I shook my legs. Then I would sway from side to side. Then I added a little shoulder shaking. In the meantime, many of the older women from my audiences would come up to me and offer their advice – "Shake them hips honey" "Don't be afraid to gyrate that pelvis" and "It's okay to do the bump and grind." It wasn't long before many of the moves were just happening spontaneously, and when I came off stage, I couldn't even remember what I did. I was just reacting to the audience and we were all having a great time.

The band played together and drew large crowds for over a year. I didn't do a lot of dancing with that band because I had to play rhythm guitar and sing backup vocals on most songs. I also learned more about singing harmony with the guys during this time period. God sure was good in surrounding me with excellent performers that taught me tricks of the trade. I learned a lot in a very short timeframe by working with these seasoned musicians. The guys in the band were also leery of letting me do too many Elvis songs because they were afraid it would drive some people away. We did a large cross section of musical styles and we needed to keep things mixed up all the time. So, it was several years before I was able to perfect all the Elvis dance moves that I still do today.

My Journey In The Shadow of "The King"
........From Graceland to the Promised Land

That first winter after graduating from high school I met someone while the Variations were performing at a local bowling alley lounge. I dated her for about seven months and we got married at the tender age of 19. Since I was entertaining full time when I met her, and before we got married, I told her that I planned to be a FULL time entertainer. She agreed. (She later renigged on this agreement.)

After we got married, I moved out of the apartment with Franky. My new wife and I moved into our own apartment in the North end of Saginaw. The band ultimately broke up and I struck out on my own as a soloist and began singing as a single act 5-6 nights a week in Saginaw and in Detroit every week. I would get a few shows here and there from Al Cole, but it wasn't enough to pay all my bills. I found some of my own jobs, but, all of the nights were just me and my guitar. Some nights I would sing two hours in Saginaw then drive to Detroit and sing five more hours there! I sang seven hours a day, just me and my guitar.

I was so driven to make a career as a full time entertainer, I was willing to do just about anything to keep singing. The way I found one singing job in Saginaw was quite unique:

I was driving one afternoon and remembered there was a club near downtown Saginaw that had a sign advertising entertainment. I stopped by to ask if I could meet the owner-manager – and as *luck* would have it - he was sitting at the bar! (Actually luck had nothing to do with it, it was ALL directed by God and His overall plan for my life.) When I asked him if he needed entertainment for his club he said he already had nighttime entertainment. But he asked if I was any good. I said that I had my guitar in the car and could show him if he had a few minutes to listen. (I ALWAYS had my guitar with me and was ready to sing for ANYBODY that would listen!)

He smiled and said, "Show me what you got."

So I quickly ran out and got my guitar and sang several songs for him. He immediately offered me a job from 5pm-7pm for their happy hour on Wednesday-thru-Friday. When I finished with that job on Thursday and Friday afternoons, I would drive to Detroit and perform at another club – just me and my guitar – from 9pm-2am. That was seven hours of solo singing with nearly two hours of driving in between! I was glad that I got those "vocal lessons" a couple of years earlier. They sure came in handy during this time of my life!

After about a year at this pace, I got some sort of pneumonia and became deathly ill (no doubt from exhaustion). The illness became so intense at one point, I could not even pick my head up from my pillow. Being a self-employed entertainer, I did NOT have any medical insurance, so I just stayed home in my apartment and tried to get better. I almost died. My wife had a job at Michigan Bell Telephone in Saginaw, but since we were just newly married, I was not covered by her insurance yet.

During this time, I prayed a lot to God – to understand what was going on with my life. I worried about providing for my future kids and what the entertainment lifestyle would mean for them. I realized that if I couldn't sing – I made NO MONEY! During the end of my illness, I was starting to feel better and an Encyclopedia Salesman knocked at our door and convinced me that my future family needed a set of encyclopedias. I bought a set on a time-based payment plan and immediately took a job with American Educator as an encyclopedia salesman. Within three months, I quickly became the top seller and *won* my set of encyclopedias in a contest. We never had to pay for them! It seemed that whatever God brought my way I was able to excel at it. This interim job was very helpful at the time. When God opens a door – walk through it. If it's meant to be, it will work out for you. You never know where it might lead you. Just be sure to praise Him and give Him the glory.

My Journey In The Shadow of "The King"
........From Graceland to the Promised Land

One night in the spring of 1973 while I was out on a sales appointment in Lansing, I was driving back to my hotel room and it was dark and very rainy. I sensed a presence outside my driver's window and when I looked I saw a hand waving around the location of my rear view mirror. I heard a voice inside my head say, *It's OK. Everything is alright now.* It sounded like my Grandma Josie, who had been sick with cancer and bedridden for the past several months. Sure enough, about 20 minutes later, when I got to my hotel room there was a message for me that Grandma had died about the time I had my "visit."

She was one of the most wonderful people I had ever known. I was her first grandson and we had a VERY special bond. She was always there for me – listening, talking, encouraging, and just loving on me like nobody else. When she died, I was crushed – she never got to see my kids (they weren't born yet).

It was a long and solemn drive back to Saginaw the next day. All through the next few days I was dazed and couldn't shake the feeling about how short life was and how unfair it was to lose loved ones before you were ready to let them go. Of course, all the Italian relatives were highly emotional. There was a LOT of crying and moaning over Grandma's death; she was only 57 years old. But then during the eulogy at the Catholic Church, one of my other Detroit cousins, Brother Gabriel, who was a Capuchin Monk, exposed a surprising "secret" about being saved: Josie was in Heaven – no more suffering – no more pain. Brother Gabriel said he was jealous of Josie, he still had pains and struggles every day. Josie was in Paradise with Jesus and we should be glad for her!!! This was an eye-opening declaration for me. As a result of this revelation, I never looked at death the same way again!

My Journey In The Shadow of "The King"
........From Graceland to the Promised Land

About 6 months later, I had a couple of job opportunities open up.

I could either join GM at Saginaw Steering Gear or I could join Michigan Bell Telephone (Ma Bell). The problem with the Ma Bell job opening was that it was traditionally a woman's job as an Information Operator. It only paid $98.00 a week – where the GM job was paying $250-$300 per week. There were also outside lineman jobs at Ma Bell paying $350 a week to start, but there were no openings for *me* at this time because they usually hired men from inside transfers. But, at that time, they were hiring *women* for the non-traditional job quotas.

I found out through a friend of my wife's inside Ma Bell that after just 6 months on the job as an Information Operator, I would be eligible to transfer to the Lineman job. After seeking some inside counsel about GM from my new father-in-law who was a GM supervisor himself, I learned that at GM unless you had a degree from college, you would always remain a factory line worker. They did NOT usually promote from the ranks and they did not have a college tuition program like Ma Bell had. In fact, Ma Bell was quite well known for encouraging their employees to get an education and then get promoted into management. I decided to join Ma Bell.

> ### Looking Ahead vs. Immediate Gratification
>
> *"This became a major life lesson for me as I grew older... Don't just get stuck in a rut thinking that wherever you are in life is all that there is available to you."*

My Journey In The Shadow of "The King"
........From Graceland to the Promised Land

As I look back on it, this was another place that God not only provided opportunities, He also provided the wisdom of a multitude of counsel as He instructs us to do in Proverbs. It was a bit of a downgrade for me to give up all my entertaining money – I was making over $350-$500 a week – for a $98.00 a week job which even grew smaller after they took out the taxes! But, I had a plan. I had health benefits starting immediately; and I could see a clear future ahead of me. Little did I know how much Ma Bell would do for my family and my music career both! And I was also able to continue to sing on the side. This became a very interesting aspect of my life as I actually had *two* careers going at the same time. This became a major life lesson for me as I grew older. I was able to share this concept with my other musical friends – although most of them ignored it. You see, there are a million ways to make a million dollars; and they are not all mutually exclusive. That is to say, you can do more than one thing at a time if you have the focus and faith in yourself (and of course, God). Don't just get stuck in a rut thinking that wherever you are in life is all that there is available to you.

I quickly learned the aspects of the new corporate job. Some portions required memorization – something that my singing and acting skills had already prepared me for. Within a few short weeks, I was one of the fastest answering operators on the floor. But, I have to confess that the Information Operator job was one of the most restricting jobs I ever remember having. This was due to the nature of the work – answering thousands of calls per hour; we had absolutely NO freedom. I mean we had to sit down with our headset on and remain plugged into the main console to answer phone calls at ALL times. If you needed to use the rest room, you had to place a card on your little glass wall and wait for a supervisor's assistant to come by and give you permission to leave. Then they watched you to be sure you were back in five minutes or less. It was like being in a prison at times.

They scheduled *every* minute of your work tour. Sometimes you would be scheduled for 8 full hours straight. Other times you got a split-shift – four hours in the morning and four hours in the evening. It was crazy. No wonder people transferred out of there or quit so often. But, I was on a mission – I knew my plans and I was excited about the next six months.

My Journey In The Shadow of "The King"
........From Graceland to the Promised Land

My supervisor was very pleased with my progress and I received several commendations during my short stay in Operator Services. You should have seen her face when I asked for a meeting with her to discuss my upcoming transfer:

"How do you know you can transfer?" She boldly challenged me.

"I talked with Flo from HR and she gave me all the details." I innocently replied.

"Well, we don't just let people go this quickly after starting here", she replied.

"According to HR, I have a right to transfer on my 6-month anniversary – and I am applying for a lineman job," I proclaimed.

There was nothing she could do about it and she knew it. But, she sure didn't like it. They had made a practice of keeping the newbies in the dark about the transfer policies.

The most incredible thing about the whole situation was that my 6-month anniversary fell on December 25th and as of January 1st (just seven days later) they changed the transfer guidelines to 18 months! Wow! How great is our God!!! Another year in there would have been horrible for me! I can honestly say that I might have quit and switched over to GM if that had been the case.

Meanwhile, I was getting only a few calls for entertainment bookings from Al Cole and the measly $98.00 paychecks were making things rough at home; we literally could only afford to spend $10.00 a week on groceries for the two of us – and I even took my lunch to work! Money was very tight, so all the entertaining I could get was a huge help.

It seems there was a hunger for Elvis music in the years 1973-1977 even before Elvis died. People were pleased with my God-given singing abilities. It was during this time period I also learned to wiggle a little more each year until I was flat out dancing and gyrating up a storm. I don't know exactly how or when it all came together, but I do remember watching every Elvis movie that came out in the movie theaters or that came on television. I also learned a lot from all the individual shows I was doing. But it wasn't all about dancing and teasing the audience. I just loved to sing and watch people get enjoyment from my efforts.

There was one night in particular at the Holiday Inn in Midland when I was performing alone on my guitar in the lounge. It was a weeknight and there was a decent-sized crowd, but they were *very* quiet. I was used to a more upbeat audience, especially when I did my Elvis music. But, this night there were a lot of business men and they were pretty low key. During one of my breaks I sauntered up to the bar and ordered my traditional Coca-Cola – I NEVER drank alcohol when I was performing. An elderly gentleman sitting next to me looked over at me and said,

"Nice job. You're a really good singer."

I sheepishly replied: "Well you couldn't tell it from this crowd. They're so quiet. In between songs, you could hear a pin drop in here."

He smiled one of the wise old man smiles and very gently answered back "Did you ever stop to think the reason they are so quiet is that they don't want to miss anything?"

WOW. What a revelation for a young 20-something performer. I never looked at audiences the same way again. Because I love to sing so much, I ALWAYS sang my heart out for every performance. I had come to expect a loud rousing ovation at the end of my songs. Now, I learned that *some* audiences show their appreciation in different ways.

That message was an eye opener for me – and was actually very freeing. Now I was no longer bound by what *I* perceived the audience reaction should be. Now I would just do my best and leave the rest in God's hands. Yes, I said God's hands – because when you do your best and give Him the rest, YOU – yourself - can rest in the fact that He will deal with you and them. Then you can move forward and not carry all the responsibility yourself. This is a major truth for life in general as well as on the stage. We cannot control the reactions of others – and we should not blame ourselves when people do, or don't do, what we think they should do. When you understand and employ this concept in your life, it is VERY freeing.

> WHATEVER YOU DO, DO IT HEARTILY, AS TO THE LORD AND NOT TO MEN. COLOSSIANS 3:23

I ultimately formed my own band called "Yellow Munday" with Tom Kissel, Rich Carlson and a couple other players. We played together for about 2 years. It was with this band that I learned another valuable lesson: the audience is a reflection of the energy that the band puts out...the band isn't supposed to wait until the crowd gets excited first.

This is what led me to discover this valuable lesson: One Friday night after we finished our first set, my band was feeling pretty down because the audience was absolutely dead. I told them to watch me closely and follow my lead when we went back out after our first break of the evening. (We had three more hours to go with these turkeys!) When we went back out, we started with a high energy song and then did two more until we had every person in the place hollering or singing along. I acted like I just won the lottery and we were all going to share the spoils! People just lit up and responded almost immediately to this change in attitude. After that set, the band was overwhelmed –

"What the heck just happened out there?" they said.

I told them that we weren't supposed to get inspired by the audience, they were waiting for US to light their fire! They had worked all day and were looking for an escape from all their problems. After I taught this lesson to my band we had many great performances together.

Once again, this is a lesson for life as well as the stage. When we get down and drag ourselves around the house or act droopy around our friends, it also drags others down. We need to call on God and remember how much He loves us – He's always there for us. It reminds me of the account in Acts 16 verses 20-26 of how Paul and Silas were beaten and put in prison with shackles on their feet (now *there's a reason to mope*) – but they didn't whine and complain. No. They prayed and sang hymns to God. Do you know what happened next? God sent an earthquake that shook the jail and burst their shackles and opened their cell doors.

What an awesome God that, while we were still disobedient sinners – He STILL sent His son to die for us. My friends, if you don't get excited when you think about being with Christ in Paradise – even though you don't deserve to – then you still don't understand the Gospel of Christ our Messiah!

DON'T MOPE.

CALL OUT TO GOD.

HE LISTENS AND ANSWERS.

Acts 16:20-26

All the while I was performing on weekends with this band, I continued to work at Ma Bell and got promoted to a job as an outside lineman and then as a supervisor in the computer department. I had been working for a couple years outside with several other guys and a couple of women. This was when there was a big push for women to perform non-traditional jobs and we had two that wanted to learn how to climb telephone poles. One of the guys on the crew hated working with them – so he would harass them and make them do extra work. One day, when he was being mean to one of the women, I just popped; I couldn't sit by and watch him bring her to tears and not do something about it. While he was snacking on some doughnuts, a piece dropped on the floor, I spoke up and said, "Wow, I don't know how you did it, but you missed your mouth!" Everybody got real quiet.

Then I said, "What's your problem always picking on Wanda?" "She hasn't done anything to you. Why don't you pick on somebody your own size?" (He was twice as big as her...maybe from all those doughnuts.) I was learning how to be a team player.

In my band, I also had to learn how to get things done through others – because the other band members would often complain behind my back; they were afraid to tell me stuff directly because I could fire them.

At Ma Bell, I made some great publicity connections for my entertaining when the internal company newspaper was looking for articles on employees that did unique things – like imitate Elvis...This was an incredible boost for my entertainment career because at the time there were over 40,000 employees from all over Michigan that received this paper at their homes. So every time they did an article on me (Four in all over 15 years) more and more people from different towns would contact me and want me to do shows and events for them. They also followed my career via a new fan club that was formed (even though I was not totally in favor of it...it felt weird).

Here's where my music career took another step up to becoming more professional: There was a local accountant woman who saw me perform for an office party that her boss put on. She was related to the manager that hired me into the band that brought me to Saginaw: *The Variations*. Anyway, Fran was a very devout Elvis fan and she told me my impersonations were excellent. She decided she wanted to make me a white Elvis-style jumpsuit. (Fran was also an excellent seamstress.) My wife was totally against it and was *very* jealous and suspicious of Fran's intentions. So we blew her off by stating that we couldn't afford to spend the extra money on all the materials for a fancy jumpsuit. Besides, I NEVER really wanted to pretend I actually *was* Elvis, I just liked singing his songs.

My Journey In The Shadow of "The King"
........From Graceland to the Promised Land

Fran was married and her husband understood his wife's passion for Elvis, so he actually called me around the Thanksgiving holiday that year and asked me what size belt I wore. So I answered him. Then he asked my shirt size and sleeve length. Now, he was getting a little too personal – so I asked him why he wanted to know. He said his wife wanted to make me the jumpsuit as a Christmas present. There would be absolutely no cost to me. So, I agreed and within six weeks I owned my first white Elvis jumpsuit.

It was about this time that I began to branch out and joined another SHOW Band called "The Sidewalkers" with Roger Walker (who did Johnny Cash and Dean Martin impersonations) Bill Herald, Marty Viers and Gary Smith. This band was *phenomenal*, we drew standing-room-only crowds for many years!

Danny with the Sidewalkers

The very first time I wore my new white jumpsuit was with the Sidewalkers at the Roaring Twenties Night Club in Saginaw, Michigan in 1976. You should have heard the audience reaction when I came out on stage in that white jumpsuit. You would have thought Elvis himself had just walked out! It was unbelievable! And I have to tell you that I felt like a different person when I was on stage with that jumpsuit – I can't fully explain it – except to say that when those people began to scream and applaud with such enthusiasm – my adrenalin jumped, I was pumped, and my whole body shook so my efforts escalated with their ovations! The show was an instant success and we brought the house down. Just a few months later, on August 16, 1977 we got the terrible news that Elvis died..........

I was driving in my car, running errands that day when I turned on my radio and they were talking about Elvis. I listened for a few minutes and had a strange feeling come over me. *"Why are they talking about Elvis in the past tense?"* I asked myself. And then the announcer said – Elvis was found dead in his Graceland Mansion. What a shock! Then I started feeling a little guilty – all these years I had thought about how far my own career might be able to go except that Elvis was there overshadowing me and many others performers. I guess it was a form of jealousy – and my Mom had often warned me about my conceit level!

"There isn't any conceit in our family." She would say… "YOU'VE got it all!" Then she would laugh out loud with her contagious laugh. It gave me a complex for a lot of years. But, I finally figured out that she actually did me a favor. When you entertain and people think you are good – it really can go to your head. That's where many entertainers lose it – and become prima donnas – thinking they are royalty and the world needs to cater to their every whim!

Danny
with
Slick Gordon & the Greasers

I quickly got over my guilt complex about Elvis when the crowd at the Roaring Twenties started calling for an Elvis song the day after he died. I COULDN'T DO IT! I was afraid to sing his songs anymore. I wore all black that weekend and made a vow to honor Elvis' memory by NOT doing any of his songs on our show. We did everything else, Johnny Cash, Dean Martin, Don Ho, The Temptations and our favorite – "Slick Gordon & the Greasers."

For several weeks, the audience kept calling for Elvis. I didn't know what to do. I thought that by putting on the jumpsuit and doing his songs, I was disrespecting him; especially so soon after he died.

One night the crowd was VERY restless… "Elvis….Elvis…Elvis!" they cried over and over again. Finally, the club owner, Rose Gaertner called me over to her office and said, "You better do some Elvis or this mob is going to destroy the place."

I reluctantly agreed to do a couple Elvis songs, and WOW – the place exploded with screams and applause! Two weeks later, we did a full Elvis show with the white jumpsuit and it was standing room only with 30-40 people standing in the foyer trying to strain their necks to get a peak! It was unbelievable. And, I have to confess, it was both awkward and awesome at the same time. I still wasn't sure that I should be doing Elvis – especially in a jumpsuit…but, the crowd was obviously sure that *THEY* wanted it!

So, in order to clear my conscience, I made a brief speech – starting that night at the Roaring Twenties – I said, *"Ladies and gentlemen. I know that I am not Elvis. He can never be replaced. My name is Danny Vann and I am a fellow Elvis fan here to do a respectful Salute to the man - that I believe - was the Greatest entertainer the world has ever known."*

You could have heard a pin drop as I was making that declaration – but, when I finished – the ovation was thunderous! And that speech became an intricate part of all of my performances from 1977 to this day! And I REALLY mean every word of it!

My Journey In The Shadow of "The King"
........From Graceland to the Promised Land

became a daddy in November 1977 when my son, Troy Joseph, was born. And again in September 1980 when Shannon Lynn joined the family. As they were growing up, I spent lots of time with the kids. I also worked at Ma Bell and continued to entertain.

This was a very interesting time for me, I was doing very well and had been promoted into management at Ma Bell – and my music career also seemed to prosper. This was the period when both my careers really began to blossom. Al Cole and several other agents around Michigan booked me to perform a lot of specialty shows – sometimes up to 60 shows a year; all over the state. I was VERY-VERY busy – but, I loved every minute of it! There were many fans, many shows, many bands and even many standing ovations. I was doing all kinds of publicity interviews for radio, TV and even for a new book about Elvis impersonators – which they wound up titling "I Am Elvis" (I might not have participated if I had known the final title....)

Around 1978 one of my fans, Fran A., started a Fan Club for me. Even though there was a lot of attention on me, I still made sure to give God credit for it all. I would frequently sing gospel songs like *Amazing Grace* or *How Great Thou Art* at my performances. Like Elvis, I loved these songs – and the audience responded very well when I sang them.

Unfortunately, there were some struggles at home with differences my wife had about all the singing I was doing and my need to go to church EVERY Sunday. Through it all, I persevered and followed my heart. I just loved to sing and that's what I did! For me, there was never any feeling quite like being on stage, singing a song and getting a rousing ovation from hundreds (sometimes thousands) of people. Unlike corporate America, the satisfaction when you are on stage is immediate. You can feel the energy and the results of your efforts can be seen in the eyes, voices and applause of the audience.

It was during this time that I began expanding my song routine. I had learned many things from watching other entertainers at all the floor shows Al Cole booked for me. Roger Walker from the Sidewalkers was so natural on stage and had the ability to capture the audience and keep their attention. He reminded me of a singer that had a brief TV show in the 1970's– Tony Orlando – who came out on stage and just mesmerized everyone. I experimented with all these various methods and ultimately learned to be very responsive to whatever was going on in my audience while I was on stage. This caused the audience to be VERY attentive and responsive to my every move. Hey – they NEVER knew what I was going to do next (neither did I). That's what made it even more fun! And when I would jump off the stage during my performances and sing and wander through the audiences shaking hands, there was an even greater response and a deeper connection with the crowd.

I remember performing at the Saginaw Moose one time just before they moved me from a 20-minute side act to the full headliner doing two full 40-minute shows per night. When I walked into the club that night, the crowd roared and gave me a standing ovation. Folks, I had not done anything except just walk into the club! Then at show time the exotic dancer came out and after five minutes into her routine the crowd started shouting – "ELVIS-ELVIS – we-want-Elvis."

I was so embarrassed – I waved my hands to settle the crowd down and watch the show. Then when I finally did my show, they wouldn't let me quit. They kept calling for an encore. They would give me a 10-minute standing ovation and kept calling for more. It actually got kind of scary at one point; we thought we might have a riot on our hands. But, eventually they quieted down and the club manager announced that the bar would close in a few minutes and this was the last call to order final drinks.

My Journey In The Shadow of "The King"
........From Graceland to the Promised Land

Eventually, the Saginaw Moose made me a solo act and increased my pay. I even performed for the annual statewide Moose convention a couple of times.

In the meantime, Ma Bell's newspaper, called the Tie Lines, continued doing articles on my singing adventures. It was after one of these interviews that they took a picture of me with my guitar for the paper – and when I saw it, I was very shocked at how curly and frizzy my hair looked (compared to Elvis' straight hair). I thought if I was going to be a *serious* Elvis Impersonator, I better look the part to the best of my ability. So after some serious deliberations with several friends and relatives, I decided to get an Elvis wig. During that time there were very few Elvis impersonators (just a handful in all of Michigan) so there was no place to go and get an "Elvis" styled wig. I had to go to a beauty shop and find a wig with hair like his and get it cut and styled. It was a long, and expensive, process. But it paid off in the end. What a difference it made in my appearance and my shows. I felt more confident when wearing it, although it was not without its quirks.

As I was preforming at the Saginaw Moose one Saturday night – I jumped up in the air to do my usual splits and lost my balance and fell right on my butt. When I did, my wig popped off...and the crowd roared with laughter. So I just ran my hands through my real hair and messed it all up and finished the show without the wig. It turned out to be quite liberating. I began to realize that the audience didn't seem to mind what my hair looked like – whether I had a wig or my real hair. I had considered straightening my real hair, but I really didn't want to go to my daytime job looking like Elvis all day. It was bad enough that I had the Elvis mutton-chop sideburns.

One day I received a call from some folks wanting to do a fundraiser for my old alma-mater – Handy High School in Bay City. The music program was in need of some funding to help send the band to a training camp and they asked if I would consider doing an Elvis concert to help raise money. Of course, I was ecstatic about the idea of doing such a concert back on my home turf. I asked Fran A if she could make me a custom jumpsuit with my high school colors of red and white for the special occasion. She said *yes!*

My Journey In The Shadow of "The King"
........From Graceland to the Promised Land

My new suit wound up being an all-red suit with the sleeves lined with white long and dangly fringe. The belt was made of red and white macramé. It was all patterned after a suit similar to one Elvis wore on stage for his touring concerts in 1969-70. It turned out to be a great concert and I made sure to do many of the songs I had learned in Handy's music room – like *All Shook Up, Don't Be Cruel, Your Cheatin' Heart* and of course, *Amazing Grace*.

It was a successful concert and I was honored to help local kids with their music goals. Getting a new jumpsuit was a great benefit for me too! I wound up wearing this suit again about a couple years later for another big concert in Bay City at the annual Fourth of July celebration. They wanted me to be the headliner at their new outside band shell at Wenona Park. I was even presented a key to the city by the mayor – Ann Hatchel. We recorded a *live* album during that concert called **LIVE: Exploding from the World Friendship Shell July 4, 1982**. It was a big seller for many years at our souvenir table. Things were definitely looking up in my show-business career.

Many other opportunities began opening up as well. I even did some inside winter shows at many malls around Michigan and Illinois. The Fashion Square Mall show in Saginaw was quite memorable because on the day of my show it was -20 F outside and even the windows inside the mall were all frosty from the bitter cold. Everyone's nerves were on edge as we approached show time that day, the band braved the cold and we were all set up and warmed up...then we waited in hopes that the crowd to show up...AND THEY DID! In record numbers. The management, as well as all the band members were amazed, and we sure had a great time. I wore two different costumes – a faux black leather two-piece suit like the one Elvis wore in his 1968 Comeback Special on NBC – and a white jumpsuit.

My Journey In The Shadow of "The King"
........From Graceland to the Promised Land

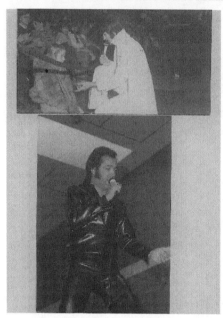

Figure 7: Fashion Square Mall - Saginaw, MI

The strangest thing happened to me when I was wearing the black leather suit....as I was singing *It's Now or Never,* I usually jump up in the air at the end of the second chorus and do a splits....and then stand up and finish the last stanza of the song. Well, after my splits, as I was finishing the song, the crowd started oooo-ing and awwww-ing real loud. Then, all of a sudden I felt a draft in my groin....when I looked down to check it out, there was a LOUD roar as the crowd watched me discover that I had split the crotch in my leather pants. But, without missing a beat, I quickly crossed my legs – while still singing mind you – and I sat down on my guitar player's amplifier and finished the song....and at the very end I dropped to my knees to take my bow. Again there was a loud roar from the crowd and very long ovation for the song. I grabbed a towel from the stage and backed away from the audience and went into the nearby Tuxedo Store and borrowed a pair of black pants and finished the show.

We shattered attendance records there that day and on several return visits. We did the same at other malls in Michigan and at the Cherryvale Mall in Rockford, Illinois. Those were some adventurous times and long road trips too.

As the word about my shows and their success began to spread, we got calls to do shows all over the state of Michigan. We also made calls to various festivals on our own: there was the Raisin Fest in Bellevue near the Raisin River, the Strawberry Fest in Ypsilanti, Potato Festival in Munger, the Sugar Beet Festival in Sebewaing, and the Dodge City Days festival up in

My Journey In The Shadow of "The King"
........From Graceland to the Promised Land

Harrison, Michigan. This was one of my favorites, they even had a portable jail and a six-shooter gun fight at high noon. If you didn't buy a charity pin for the day, the sheriff would lock you up until somebody bought you one to bail you out! I only got locked up once to learn my lesson! We returned there for a period of almost 10 years. The crowds grew year-by-year until there were over 1,000 people attending at the height of the festival's popularity. I was told that this was quite a crowd for such a rural area.

The Dodge City Days festival was a two-day event held on the grounds behind the volunteer fire department building. The music we provided was for four-hours per night. The band did a dance set – then I did my first Elvis Show – then another dance set and the end of the evening was my second Elvis show. By this time I had over six custom-made Elvis suits. I had two white ones, my original white with Blue, and the White American Eagle suit like he wore at the Aloha Concert. I also had the Red & White fringe, a Powder Blue with Silver Swirl, and a Black suit with silver studs. Finally, the Black Leather (with new real-leather pants that couldn't split).

It got to the point that I had to write down which suit I wore each year so that I didn't repeat myself. I also tried to make sure we mixed up the song lists for return shows to keep the crowds interested every year. Although over the years I found out that there were many songs that they *wanted to hear every year*, like, *Jailhouse Rock, Teddy Bear, Love Me Tender, Don't Be Cruel, In the Ghetto, American Trilogy* and of course, *How Great Thou Art.*

They brought in a temporary stage. It was a long tractor trailer for us to stand on so the crowd could see us more clearly. The event was on a grassy lot of a couple acres and was usually dry since it was held in mid-July.

One year it was a very rainy summer and they had a huge mosquito problem, so, unknown to me, they sprayed the grounds with some sort of repellant. It turned out that I was allergic to whatever it was they used. By the end of my second show on Friday night, I began to become hoarse – I almost never got hoarse from singing. When I woke up the next morning I could barely talk – all that came out was squeaks…..that's when I found out about the overspray they used in the field before we arrived. I was told that they expected a huge crowd for the Saturday night shows – what was I going to do? I could barely talk – let alone sing for over two hours!!! So, I remembered that my new friend, Tommy Durden lived over in Houghton Lake, not too far from Harrison. I called him and asked him to come over and help me do the show for the night! He agreed – and said he was honored to share the stage with me again. We sure had a good time that night and even though I was a squeaky Elvis, it seemed everybody was satisfied with both shows! What an exciting adventure!

For several of the years at Dodge City Days, my dad even showed up and we were able to recognize him and his wife, Betsy, for helping buy me my first guitar. It was at these shows that I was also proud to dedicate Dad's favorite song, *Wooden Heart*, to him. It was fun to watch the festival staff pamper him like they did to me. (Even though I did not demand it, they always treated me like a king!) We came a long way from that first song when Dad was reading his newspaper! It was also good to be recognized by Dad for finally making something out of my music.

Toward the end of our tenure at Dodge City Days, I was invited to perform at the Clare County Fair. In order to honor the DCD folks, I asked their permission to do the County Fair show so I didn't step on anybody's toes because the locations were so close to each other. They were glad I was able to do the big stage at the fair and permission was granted.

It turned out that there were going to be three acts on the stage that night: a comedian was to open the show, then they hired a female country artist who had also made a big name for herself locally, and finally they requested that I do my Elvis show last. Well, the female artist was very upset by their schedule – and felt that *she* should be the last act on stage. (That was usually the slot reserved for the main headliner.) When I found out about the conflict of opinion, I volunteered to perform second but, the fair managers insisted that the rotation they declared was to take place at show time with no changes.

My Journey In The Shadow of "The King"
........From Graceland to the Promised Land

When the night of the show came, and while the comedian was warming up the audience, the female artist and her band were a no-show. They finally called the fair manager and said they had a flat tire and would be over ½ hour late and that I would probably have to perform before they could arrive to set up. To me, that was not a problem. We took the stage and about the time my band did their first song (they always did 2-3 crowd pleasing songs to get the crowd going and test all the equipment and sound levels before I came out) - the female artist and her band showed up.

So I did my show and the crowd was *very* enthusiastic. We got several standing ovations throughout the show. When I finished, I went to my souvenir table and greeted the fans and signed autographs while the other band set up and started their show. By now it was getting very dark and something strange happened ...most of the audience LEFT THE FAIRGROUNDS! When one of my band members told me about it, I went into the seating area and was shocked to see only a handful of people sitting for the final performance of the night. I felt terrible for the folks on stage having to perform to an empty grandstand. I guess the lesson I learned that night is that it pays to stay humble and don't force your way on other people – it could backfire on you. It's better not to sound your own horn about your success, and if people ask you to take a back seat, do it with humility.

After every concert I performed, I would always take time to meet the fans, sign autographs and of course, shake hands with all the kids. It was like living a dream at times – but, unfortunately, Monday morning would come around every week and it was back to the corporate grind. I say unfortunately because I would *always* prefer to be singing. But, God was also very-very good to me in the corporate arena. I enjoyed being a computer analyst and then becoming a manager – solving problems and creating solutions where none appeared to be possible. I guess it was fairly close to my performing gigs, except instead of cheering fans, I usually had frowning computer clients and/or bosses who wanted problems fixed ASAP. Occasionally, we would get accolades when we installed a big project on time with no bugs (errors). But those were few and far between compared to singing.

My Journey In The Shadow of "The King"
........From Graceland to the Promised Land

Then in 1982 Ma Bell moved my job and family to the Detroit area – Southfield, MI to be exact. I was given a promotion to take a new role as billing analyst.

We moved to Canton, and I had to commute to Southfield daily. It was about a 50 mile round trip each day. That was 1,000 miles a month just to go to the daytime job. Then, when I had Elvis shows all around Detroit or in Grand Rapids, Muskegon, Standish, or in Gaylord – those were extra miles that we traveled week after week. It seems I was also "blessed" with a road-warrior lifestyle like my dad.

From the time I was 19 years old, I have driven an average of 30,000-40,000 miles per year on the highways of Michigan (and sometimes Ohio & Illinois) performing Elvis and commuting to Corporate America to make a living. I loved it in spite of how draining it was at times. It was a constant adventure. Just doing it at a *local* level was taxing enough on my family and me; I don't know how some of those national stars can do it on a bus or airplane – crisscrossing the country week after week. No wonder so many of them wind up burned-out and divorced!

DID YOU CATCH THAT?

I WORKED MULTIPLE JOBS ALL MY LIFE IN ORDER TO GET THINGS FOR MY FAMILY THAT WE NEVER HAD WHEN I WAS A KID.
TO SUCCEED IN LIFE YOU HAVE TO PUSH YOURSELF!

I started getting bookings to perform at Parks and Recs summer outdoor concerts all around the Detroit Metro area. What a tremendous amount of *FUN* my family and I had at these shows – even the bands loved them because they were so short compared to the nightclubs. (Two-to-three hours versus five-to-six hours - including set-up, Showtime, and teardown.)

There are several incidents that come to mind from some of those shows:

We had a very good crowd turnout at our second return visit to Shepherd Park in Oak Park, MI. The band set up and started doing their warm-up songs and then we started the Elvis portion of the show. The show was supposed to be around 75 minutes long. About two songs into the show, the power died and nobody could get it restarted. I could see the crowd was getting restless, so I told my guitar player to hand me my acoustic guitar that I used as I walked out on stage at the beginning of the show. (Like Elvis did on his concerts.) Luckily, I always tuned it up and sometimes would actually play it during CC Ryder at the beginning of the show. Well, I grabbed that guitar and jumped off the stage with it and ran into the middle of the audience and started belting out *Heartbreak Hotel* – with no microphone or backup music other than my own acoustic guitar. The crowd went WILD! I had to settle them down so they could hear me singing! Then I sang *Blue Suede Shoes* and was starting into *Hound Dog* when the power was finally restored! The audience gave me a standing ovation as I made my way back up on stage. My agent told me the following year when they re-booked the show, that the community was still talking about that intimate Elvis concert when the power went out! What a FUN time – and I was glad that God gave me the ability to learn to play guitar and sing at the same time.

Are you noticing a repeating theme here? We were all having FUN at these concerts. The audience, the band, my family – and ME! I studied and practiced for years doing the thing that I loved to do and God made a way that I could continue doing it. And I got paid for it!!!! How cool is that?

Another time we were in Detroit's downriver area for another summer concert and the Parks and Rec Manager gave us strict orders to be finished by 9:45pm – because they were going to start fireworks! He said they would stop the show and start the fireworks if we were not done (this is awesome)... of course we watched the clock diligently during the whole show. When we came to the final song of the show, it was time to finish with my favorite ending – *How Great Thou Art*. So we hurried to get the song started – it was going to be close, but we were sure we could squeeze it in. As I came to the VERY LAST line of the song where the notes go VERY high....HOW....G-R-E-A-T .T-H-O-U.......KABOOOM!!!! The first explosion came on the last word – ART! How great was the ending to that song as the people were already focused on God during the very emotional concert rendition. And to have the explosion at the precise time of the last word was uncanny. My band and I talked about that one for a long time as well.

Then another "Dodge Park" came into focus for us. This time it was in Sterling Heights, MI. One of my many agents arranged for me to do a trial backup tape concert show in Sterling Heights at a park called Dodge Park. I did the show and they had a very good turnout for my show. They asked me back again the following summer – this time with my band...and voila – a new legacy began!

Something very interesting happened that first year: in between my two shows, somebody came up and challenged me saying,

"That's not really YOU singing – it's really Elvis and you are just mouthing the words" (this was BEFORE Karaoke came along).

I quickly met the challenge and said, "It REALLY is me and I can prove it. What's your name? I will sing your name during the next show so you can know it is a LIVE microphone and that I am really singing."

So, I did it - and later they came back and expressed their amazement. I gave God all the credit for this, because He gave me the voice, I just learned how to use it as best as I could. That was the beginning of a whole new routine that I added to my act from that day forward. Even with the live band, I always injected words, names, towns and other comical comments during some of the songs on the show to prove it was really ME doing the singing on the microphone. It turned out to be quite popular with the audiences – they liked hearing their city mentioned during the songs!

My Journey In The Shadow of "The King"
........From Graceland to the Promised Land

Be Flexible

You'll be surprised how much fun it is to "overcome" trials instead of resisting or grumbling about them.

I started to go into the audience during *Love Me Tender* or *I Can't Help Falling* or *My Way* – to shake hands, and I would also make a lot of comments and talk to people over the microphone to make the show more personable. I learned that being flexible both on stage and in my daytime job was a very good thing for me and those around me. It doesn't pay to get mad about events out of your control – just take a deep breath and pause to give God a chance to inspire you, and move forward with a positive attitude. You'll be surprised how much fun it is to *overcome* trials instead of resisting or grumbling about them.

From our second year and onward at Dodge Park in Sterling Heights we broke attendance records every year for nearly ten years. The crowds just kept getting bigger and bigger. Of course, it helped that they had their own cable TV station which came out and recorded the concert and then played it throughout the year. At one time they told me it was the most requested concert on their broadcast. We wound up being the headliners for their main event every summer – called Sterling Fest which included an oldies car show with many food vendors and arts & crafts as well. These shows were especially dear to me because there were so many kids attending. I started giving out little teddy bears to the kids – sometimes a half dozen during the song *Let Me Be Your Teddy Bear*. I would call all the kids up to the front of the stage and make them all sit down – experience taught me that if they were standing when I threw the bears some of the little kids could get trampled. So after they sat down, I would tell them that they MUST be good and not steal a bear from someone else – because there were over 2,000 eyeballs watching them (from the 1,000+ people in attendance). The looks on their tiny faces during the song and teddy bear tossing were just priceless. Then before the song was over, I would jump off the stage and shake the hand of EVERY child that wanted to meet me. It was so precious. I have to tell you that these were some of the best moments of my entertaining career – and I was really having fun doing these outside – family-friendly – concerts. I would tell everyone around me that I was really having FUN Being ME (and Elvis).

In 1983, at 30 years old, I began to wonder about life: why were there so many problems and pains? Why was there so much suffering? Why were some newborn babies born handicapped, while others came out perfect? Where was God in all this mess?

RELIGIOUS QUEST

... nobody could answer the deeper questions – except to repeat over and over "God knows best" – or "it's not for us to know all these things at this time...

I sought answers from our Lutheran ministers, Catholic Priests, other ministers and spiritual leaders, and nobody seemed to be able to answer all of these questions completely for me. Then one day, after spending weeks debating and sharing thoughts on God, the universe, and spirituality with a neighbor, Don C, he brought me a book called – 'Wisdom of the Mystic Masters'. This book was a study of the Rosicrucian's – a group that studied the hidden powers of the Universe. When I started reading it, I began to see answers to **some** *of my questions unfold.*

My Journey In The Shadow of "The King"
........From Graceland to the Promised Land

It was during this time that a new personal entertainment manager, John H, came into my life. He promised me "real stardom" and guaranteed me that I should – and would – play Vegas. (And I DID – twice.) John had an astrologer do my star chart and compared it to Elvis' charts. The similarities were uncanny. He was convinced that I had all the potential to become a star like Elvis. John and I met with the astrologer, Veronica B, many times and she introduced me to an Eastern Philosophy of spirituality called Sant Mat – meaning "teachings of the saints".

At first this quest was just a spiritual question-and-answer session with my neighbor, Don. But, after meeting Veronica and reading most of the book on Wisdom of the Mystic Masters, I became very intrigued with what I was learning about God and man's relationship with Him. I spent months reviewing material about the Eastern Philosophy. I even met with a couple of priests and our Lutheran Minister to discuss the differences. Again, nobody could answer the deeper questions – except to repeat over and over "God knows best" – or "it's not for us to know all these things at this time." Which to me, were cop-out answers. So, I began going to local Sant Mat meetings and increased my studies of BOTH the Bible and the new Eastern materials. At the request of our Lutheran minister, I even read the **entire** New Testament – start to finish. And there were still no answers to all of my questions. (I learned later that many answers were in the Old Testament – and that without the Holy Spirit's guidance, it's impossible to see God's Word clearly.)

After many months of investigation and study, I became a strict lacto-vegetarian and joined the local Sant Mat group in Detroit. This created a huge stress on my marriage. My wife's anger and resistance to this spiritual study was so intense, she attacked me with a kitchen knife after one of the regional meetings in 1984. That was really when the "marriage" ended. Luckily, the kids did not witness the fight and my emergency trip to the ER because it was late at night and they were asleep. I wound up with eight stiches on

My Journey In The Shadow of "The King"
........From Graceland to the Promised Land

my right hand. Due to the severity of that episode, and on my insistence, we went to marriage counseling together for a short while – then she quit going - but I went by myself for several more years. (We wound up divorced in 1994.)

Meanwhile, all during these stressful years, I spent many-many hours with Troy and Shannon; I went to their gymnastics lessons, cub scouts, girl scouts, swimming lessons and even took Karate for 3 ½ years with them. Troy excelled in his karate class and became very good and confident. He used this later in life when he joined the marines and ultimately as a Border Patrol agent.

My mom moved in with us from Bay City during part of that time too. She met her future husband while working at the local Knights Inn. After a short while, she moved out into her own place and then later on they got married.

*Figure 8 Shannon and me –
"Aura Lee"-"Love Me Tender"*

All the while I was becoming more successful at my corporate career in computers. I was promoted to Senior Programmer over the main billing program for all of Michigan's phone bills. I didn't realize it at the time, but God was blessing BOTH of my careers at the same time. This allowed us to do many things that I had never done as a child growing up.

The kids and I were very close and spent lots of time together – including work at my shows. Shannon actually performed with me on stage several times! I remember when she came home with her saxophone and showed me that she learned how to play *Aura Lee* – it was the exact melody of *Love Me Tender* – the first song that *I* learned to play on my guitar. What a coincidence!

My Journey In The Shadow of "The King"
........From Graceland to the Promised Land

Of course, I coached her to get good enough to play it along with my band – and a NEW STAR was born!! I can still see her nervously standing off stage waiting to be introduced for her first solo (ever) and with dad on the big stage!

It's a good thing Elvis jumpsuits didn't have buttons up the chest – mine would have all popped off that night. She was a little shaky at first, but she did a great job – and the crowd LOVED her!

About this time the kids were old enough that they worked at my shows to help set up souvenir tables and sell things. They were always paid a nice percentage of what I took in from the sales. Some of the bigger shows required more attention and the whole family helped out. Here's where Troy had the chance to really shine – literally – he became my spotlight operator. Which was not an easy task. You see, since I was all about shaking hands and audience contact, I was *always* on the move during the shows. The supper club shows, where we needed the spotlight, were no exception. Troy learned the routine by watching it many times over the years (at the outside park shows...he didn't come to the supper club concerts until he was old enough to be there legally). Troy knew he had to keep his eyes on me at ALL TIMES because you never knew what I might do next (neither did I most of the time)...it was a spontaneous performance....if I saw someone or something interesting – boom! Sometimes I ran across the audience or dance floor to *surprise* the person and the audience. It took a special spotlight operator to keep up with all the activity during a show. And Troy became an expert!!!

I was also learning a lot about the marketing and business side of entertaining from John H. He opened my eyes to several aspects that would change things drastically for me and my family.

One of the first things he changed was the pay scale – for both me and my band members. This was a very tough one for me to swallow at the time. Up until the time John came on the scene, I had always split the money equally with the band. If the club paid us $300, and there were five of us – four band members and me – then we each made $60 dollars. To me that was fair since they owned their equipment, practiced the songs and hauled their own equipment, set it up, performed and tore it down. But John didn't see it that way: to him, I was the headliner – the people were coming to see ME – not the band.

It took me a while to come around to that way of thinking, but there were many shows that I had done over the years where John's words rang true; like the *specialty* shows with Al Cole and many other agents that I had been working with. I just never put the two concepts together before like John was doing. He also told me that effective immediately, our fee was going up! According to him, this show was Vegas quality and we should be charging accordingly.

When he first announced all of this to the band, they nearly quit! I stepped in and assured the band that they would continue to get the same or similar pay to what they were used to. The main change going forward was that if we received higher income for bigger shows, they would receive back-up band wages and not a full equal share as before. I also offered to give them bonuses at some of the larger venues due to additional rehearsals and also for their loyalty to the show.

They were still very upset about John's changes and disagreed with him. So he offered a challenge to them (and me) ....he would book *two* nights for our next show: the first night would be "band only" and the second night would be the whole show with me (Elvis) as the headliner. If the band could draw a crowd on Friday as big as the show did on Saturday, then we would consider splitting the pay equally. Since the next booking was at the Wayne Moose Lodge in the band's home territory of Westland, Michigan, (most members were from that area) they readily agreed to the challenge. They were sure they could draw a big crowd in their own hometown.

At the time I happened to live in Canton, only two miles from that Moose Lodge, and when that Friday night came, I just couldn't help but stop by around 11pm to see how things were going. As I turned the corner to go into the parking lot, I was heartbroken for the band – there were only about 20 cars in the lot. I quietly snuck into the back door and took a seat up at the bar where the band could not see me. Inside the clubroom where they were playing, the place wasn't even ¼ full – the seating capacity was around 350 people. I hung around for a while and then left.

The next night I arrived at the Moose Lodge about two hours early to drop off my gear (my jumpsuits, microphone, guitar and other things for the souvenir table) and I was shocked to see that even two hours before the first show the place was wall-to-wall packed with people standing in line waiting to get in! WOW! John was right! The band never brought up the issue of pay or popularity again – and neither did I. But, it still took me a long time to adjust to the new pay policy – it still didn't feel right to me to be treated like I was "better" than the band. I shared that feeling with John and he assured me that it wasn't that I was better than anyone; but from a business standpoint, I was the drawing card and was ultimately worth more. He said the band members could be replaced, and as long as I was out front doing my Elvis Show, the crowds would still show up. They were coming to see me, not the band.

We went on to do many quite successful concerts all around Michigan and in Detroit, like the 50th birthday concert for Elvis at the Royal Oak Music Theater in 1985. I was so blessed to be able to headline that show and to meet and sing "Heartbreak Hotel" with its author Tommy Durden. God was indeed blessing me more and more! It was around this time period that I was also inducted into the Elvis Presley Impersonators International Association Hall of Fame (EPIIA) based out of Chicago. I also learned that year that there were over a dozen Elvis impersonators in the Detroit metro area alone!!!

The Detroit Free Press decided to do a cover story for the 50th anniversary of Elvis' birth. They put a small blurb in the paper "calling all Elvii" to appear at their downtown headquarters for interviews and a photo-op (opportunity). Well, always being the one wanting to do something *DIFFERENT*, I figured that most of the guys would show up in the traditional

My Journey In The Shadow of "The King"
........From Graceland to the Promised Land

Elvis White Jumpsuits, so I wore my Black Jumpsuit with silver studs just like the one Elvis wore in concert. I also brought my black acoustic guitar that my buddy, Jimmy K, embellished in rhinestones with my name on it.

Just as I had hoped, I was the only one with an off-color suit – and the only one who brought a guitar. So they placed me in the middle of the crowd for the group picture – with my guitar proudly displaying my name "Danny Vann" in glitzy glory!!!

While we waited for our individual interviews, I played guitar and several of the guys and I had a blast singing the old Elvis hits. Then, all of sudden there was a mild rumble among the guys, it seems one of the impersonators had just declared that *He* was the real Elvis and that the guy that died in 1977 was an impersonator. Yikes! What a weird and crazy day that was for me.

I always did Elvis because I loved to sing the songs and it made people happy! But some of these guys were all-out fanatics about it. Some were standoffish. We even heard that one of the guys had plastic surgery to look more like Elvis.

That was about the last time I ever gathered with that many impersonators…it was all too weird for me.

A few years later, around 1989, we moved out to Howell and bought five acres and got two horses, a swimming pool, a pair of ATVs. We also bought a water-front lot and got a brand new mobile-home as our cottage in Coldwater, MI. This was a time of fun and games at home: for the kids especially. I spent many hours swimming with them, mostly Shannon, in our backyard above-ground pool. We also took time out to go riding horses, motorcycles and boats. But, Troy seemed to be slipping away during this time...I found out later that his Mom had something to do with that. Fortunately, as he got older, we were able to overcome it.

I had sworn that I would NEVER get divorced and put my kids through all the trauma that I went thru. I actually had a great *fear* of divorce. (When my wife discovered that, she used it against me.) Whenever she wanted to force me to do something, she would threaten to divorce me if I didn't do it, and I usually would back down.

Even though I went to counseling for over 5 years, things between us continued to erode and just get worse. Ultimately, she insisted it was me that had changed over the years (especially my religion and diet) and that she had remained the same as we were when we got married. After the knife incident the trust was totally destroyed and I was fearful of when - or if - there could be a repeat of that violent outburst. I literally slept with one eye open at night for many months. She tried to gloss it over and blamed it on her recent hysterectomy and an imbalance in her hormones; but her anger continually resurfaced for years afterward. It would flare up every time we would go to a restaurant or when the topic of meditating or a vegetarian diet came up. When we moved out to the rural Howell area, she even wanted to get a gun. She said it was to protect herself and the kids from raccoons. I told her that if she brought a gun into the house, I would immediately move out! We never talked about it again.

Chapter 11 - Divorce – self awakening

O ver the years, the stress seemed to only get worse and our relationship totally broke down. When I finally stopped going to counseling, at the last session the counselor told me that if I stayed with her he thought I was "crazy" because she was prone to life-threatening violence. I said that she only pulled a knife on me once – and he replied,

"It only takes once." He was right.

So, I finally moved out in order to spare the kids from the ongoing stress and any potential future encounter. I hated the thought that, like my parents, I failed in my marriage and was about to change the life of my children forever.

The process of my parents' divorce was very hard for my siblings and me – and I wanted to make it as easy as possible for my kids. So I moved less than 1 ½ miles away from them and wound up visiting them at school for lunch at least once a week. I did this EVERY week for 2-3 years until they finally asked me to stop coming because they were in high school – and it was no longer cool.

Around the time the divorce was final, December 1994, I was let go (downsized) from Ma Bell (with 21 ½ years' service). It was a devastating event and very hard for me to process. I expected to retire from there with a healthy pension. I became angry with corporate America and swore to never return. I was going to become a full-time entertainer again!

Earlier that year, my dad had open-heart surgery and received a five-way bypass. He was in Florida where he had moved after receiving some property from his aunt when she died. Being unemployed during that time was very fortunate because I was able to go and spend several weeks in Florida with him and my step-mom.

I actually made two trips during Dad's episodes with the pre-and-post surgery. The second trip was a driving trip with my two brothers. We had a blast spending time together during the drive. And when we got to Dad's, it was equally as much fun painting Dad's house and doing other things he needed done.

As I look back on these times, I'm really glad things happened the way they did. Once again, God works in mysterious ways. He took what looked like a really bad life situation for me, and allowed our family a chance to heal. It was an excellent time for the *brothers* to bond and share some quality time with Dad.

Back home in Michigan, it was a very depressing time in my life. I hated the loneliness and felt very guilty about the pain the kids were going through. I spent a lot of time in prayer and meditation and with my music. I began writing original songs. I also visited some long-lost musical friends in Bay City and Saginaw. It seems that when times get rough we cry out to God the loudest. This was the first time since my move to Cadillac, Michigan that I was completely alone.

I spent many waking hours in prayer and musical reflection on God and His purpose for my life. Most of the new songs I was writing focused on these issues as well as how my kids must be feeling as they dealt with their new broken home environment. I even wrote a song *with* Shannon that reflected how she was coping with being a tween-ager in all this mess. Her brother got his driver's license and she was still homebound and almost as lonely as me. It was heart-wrenching, but at least we were able to get her feelings out and into a song to help her cope. She knew that her dad had some understanding of what she was going through.

My Journey In The Shadow of "The King"
........From Graceland to the Promised Land

It was during this time that I also got a chance to go out to Arizona and visit my old guitar player friend, Juan (and his wife Cindy). While I was there, I wrote *I Hear an Angel Whispering* and *Gimme-a-Hug*. There was such a relief when the words to "I Hear an Angel Listening" came to me. I did not strategize or force them, they just flowed onto the paper – as if God was writing them through my hand. I could actually hear the flowing harp music as I wrote the words... "***I hear an angel whispering, telling me he's listening. So, everything I say and do, should be fit for an angel too.***" It was awesome to realize that God was telling me "**You are not alone**" – He sends His ministering spirits to watch over us. I later discovered that this is clearly spelled out in the Bible in the book of Psalms number 91 and verse 11. I now share this verse with many people as they go through their trials and suffering in life. I call it God's 911 (Psalm 91:11).

After they heard the words and music to the new angel song, Juan and Cindy jokingly said,

"Hey, you should write a song about us!" So I DID!

The next night as I was pondering THEIR life (as I saw it) – the song "Gimme-a-Hug" came to mind... "***Gimme-a-hug, nice and snug, Gimme-a-hug today. When you Gimme-a-hug I feel the love and you make me wanna stay.***" I had noticed that they hugged each other a lot and were always very affectionate toward each other. They were tickled and broke out in warm laughter when I played their new song for them. Juan and Cindy also encouraged me to continue to write even more songs when I went back home to Michigan.

While I was there, Juan and I drove from Phoenix to the Grand Canyon – it was a mystical – almost dream-like trip. This was a long-time dream come true for me – I had ALWAYS wanted to see the Grand Canyon. Seeing it with Juan – an old time *fun-filled* friend – made it all the more special. It was another inspiring event reminding me of how great our God is. The things He has done on this earth as well as in the heavens above are just incredible – if we just take the time to look around us and take them in. Juan also had a strong spiritual side. He was the music leader at his local church. We spent many hours on the road discussing things of God, the Bible, and my newfound Eastern Spiritual Philosophy. The trip to Phoenix was refreshing and encouraging and helped me through a very depressing and challenging time in my life. I am very grateful to God and Juan and Cindy for helping me through it.

My Journey In The Shadow of "The King"
........From Graceland to the Promised Land

During this time, Troy moved in with me and, at first, we had a pretty good relationship going. I was spending time in the recording studio bringing my new music to life. I HEAR AN ANGEL WHISPERING turned out great with its swirling harps and easy flowing strings and angelic voices. Troy even caught the bug and wrote a little song for his high-school sweetheart, so I scheduled time in the studio for him and we recorded his original song too. That was a special "musical" moment when he finally heard the end result of his efforts. We also recorded Gimme-a-Hug during that studio session.

Because he was going to be a senior in high school, the summer right after his junior year, I decided to take a *senior trip* with him -- one-on-one -- father-and-son. I booked a weekend cruise to the Bahamas leaving out of Palm Beach, Florida. We drove together from Michigan to Florida and had a great weekend on the Grand Bahama Island and on the cruise ship. The good part about that trip was that I was always with him as he explored his 17-year-old curiosities in a culture that allowed drinking at age 16. (Hey - they allowed us that privilege at age 18 in the early 1970's.) And, for the record, YES – I did get up and do a couple Elvis songs with the band. Even Troy danced to Jailhouse Rock – island style!

It was during this trip that I wrote the song *Whispering Wind* as I watched the palm trees swaying in the wind and the waves dancing in and out of the shoreline as I sat one morning overlooking Panama Beach. The wind is a mysterious force in God's hands: it can be calm and warm – or strong and violent – God is awesome.

After we got back, he began acting out and was nearly arrested because one of his friends was dealing drugs (marijuana) and Troy was viewed as a suspect too. Troy also had several minor car accidents and I suspected that a couple of them were due to drunk driving (he was only 17). Finally, I had to draw a hard line and took Troy's car away – Troy left me and moved back to his mother's and didn't speak to me or visit me for several years. Right after graduating high school, Troy joined the Marines and left home for good. He agrees that it was one of the best things that happened to him since it taught him discipline and to respect authority.

Shannon excelled in music – and was *first chair* in saxophone from the 8th grade on. In spite of all the turmoil, Shannon and I continued to communicate and she always made her weekend visits. I also attended many of her concerts when she played in band for local school events like football games. I even crashed several of her band rehearsals and brought my guitar into one of them and sang some songs (including Elvis of course). It was fun meeting her musical friends!

Prior to filing for divorce, I had gone back into counseling toward the end of my first marriage. Because I dreaded the pain of divorce so much, I had been trying to salvage it for the kids' sake if I could – and this new counselor was helping me work on my codependency and personal people-pleasing issues. After the divorce, the new counselor and I both agreed that I needed some time off of relationships until I had time to heal and determine who "Dan" really was (as opposed to who I tried to be for the other party). The plan was that I would NOT consider marriage for at least 2 years.

After being alone and separated for two years, I met my old high-school sweetheart at a concert I did in the Flint area - and we started dating. It was another fast courtship and to be honest, I was pressured into tying the knot after only 10 months. Well, I told myself that I was really separated and alone for nearly two years.....and that I had already known this woman when we were younger....but, that was not the intention of the counselor – and I knew it. In an effort to prevent myself from making another mistake, I brought this new person to meet the counselor - - - it was not the best results I had hoped for . After a couple of meetings, she decided she was NOT interested in meeting with my counselor anymore (that SHOULD have been a major RED flag to me – but, I didn't heed the warning). We wound up going to a couple other counselors (because there was no doubt we *both* needed some help – she had *just* completed a divorce as well). I remember the night before we decided to get married, she issued an ultimatum – "let's get married – or I am going to leave". I should not have buckled under the pressure, but I did, and we did (elope). Both of our families were shocked!

I'm not going to go into detail about this marriage – except to say that there were many-many pre-marital discussions and agreements about several key life issues:

1)-having children (I did NOT want anymore)

2)-my music (I was entertaining FULL time and LOVING it – and she agreed to support it)

3)-where we were going to live – (we agreed to live halfway between our two families; somewhere in Fenton or Hartland was the agreed upon target area).

Well – within 2 years, she was zero-for-three – meaning that she reversed her agreement on all three and also confessed to me that she knew she should *never* marry a man who had children by another woman – WHAT?????

I was absolutely shocked when I heard this one...she LIED to me about all *four* of these major issues! I review all this to give people a warning to not move too fast in relationships. Had I resisted the pressure to get married so fast, I might have learned these things *before* it was too late to walk away.

I made a mistake.

I left God out of this decision, and both my family and I were going to pay for it.

I spent the next 12 years trying to figure out how to live peacefully with her (and not have another marriage failure on my hands). The fear of divorce was still lingering in my mind. She ultimately drove my family away; my kids, my mother, and my siblings. She constantly nagged me about all aspects of my music career until I finally went back to corporate America. I reluctantly began to lay the music down when she threatened to divorce me over it. (Sound familiar?) She insisted that I was too old to do Elvis and should retire from music. So I semi-retired and just took occasional shows for the higher payouts.

In order to have *some* peace at home, I went along with as much of her ideas as I could tolerate, but the stress level was always *very* high around the house, and especially when my daughter came for her bi-weekly visitations. Troy had all but dis-owned me at this time. It seemed I was being denied every pleasure in life that was important to me, but at least she left my spirituality alone.

My music business began to slow down in the late 1990's because there were many more *new* Elvis impersonators cropping up, and many of my agents confessed that they didn't need (or want) to pay me such a high price when less experienced Elvis' were being accepted by the public for a lot less money. My band members were also giving me a lot of problems like their ego trips, tardiness, and drinking on many of the jobs; so I started doing more shows with back-up tapes. Karaoke had been out a while and audiences were more accepting of shows with recorded back-up music versus live musicians. I discovered that I could book more shows, have less hassles dealing with unreliable band members, and even get more money for myself.

I finally gave in and went almost totally solo act again. But, with bookings slowing down, it was clear that unless I was willing to travel around the country, I would need to get another source of income. So I finally dusted off my resume and started looking for a daytime job back in my other career – computers in corporate America.

finally landed a corporate job due to the Y2K panic, and I wound up making *1 ½ times* what I had been making at Ma Bell before they fired me! Once again things were looking up. We moved to Davison, Michigan, about 40 miles from my previous mobile home residence near my kids.

Shannon graduated high school and joined the marines too; but she went into their music program. When she came home to visit – she also stopped coming around as often – and then only for short visits. This was hard on Shannon as well as me. I tried very hard to manage this second marriage and I was determined that I was NOT going to have a *second* failure.

 **Surgery**

I was constantly under a lot of stress both at work and at home, and in the summer of 1998, I had an angina attack which led to a heart catherization and angioplasty. I wound up getting two stents in late August of that year. My kids were barely speaking to me and delayed their visits that summer. Just a few weeks after my angioplasty, my dad died of a massive coronary on September 16, 1998. When I recovered from the angioplasty surgery, at Betsy's request, I flew to Florida and spread dad's ashes along his favorite beach near St. Augustine where we used to go and take walks together. It was a VERY heavy feeling to carry Dad's ashes in my hands and let them drop on the sandy beach as I walked along dad's favorite path for the last time. This was a very sad time – yet I was relieved for Dad because he no longer suffered or was in the stressful marriage he endured for so many years.

Then of course, came the battles with the siblings over Dad's possessions and his vacation property back in Michigan. Against my will, Betsy signed the deed over to my name only. She said because I was the oldest, it was mine to do with whatever I pleased. I was undecided about what to do with it since there was NO way that six dysfunctional siblings (and their families) were going to be able share a rundown old mobile home that was not even on the water. After several years of holding onto it and paying taxes on it, I sold it, deducted my expenses and spilt the money equally between my five siblings. Of course, not everyone agreed with my methods and there was a rift in the family for many years. My youngest brother confided in me that he was impressed that I decided to share the proceeds with everyone,

"You didn't have to do that," he said, "that place was yours alone and you could have just walked off with all the money." At least someone appreciated my effort to be fair.

In the meantime I was calling out to God quite heavily in prayer and meditation to help me understand why He had spared me from the fate of my father and his younger brother, Uncle Burt. They had both died unexpectedly from chronic heart failure. Uncle Burt, at the tender age of 43, was walking down the sidewalk in Bay City and just fell down and died instantly.

Some 20+ years later, Dad was trimming trees in his back yard in Florida, went in for a glass of water, and then went out to take down his ladder. He never returned – having also fallen down and died instantly of a massive heart attack. My angina attack was a warning sign that I am grateful to have heeded – but, now what was it that God wanted me to do with the rest of my life? Why did He spare me?

All of these things made for a very tense life. In addition, I was driving many miles to work every day from Davison to Lansing. Then I got a new consulting job which had me driving from Davison to Detroit. Like my dad's marriage, this second marriage was very tense with frequent arguments and even though I went to counseling with my wife for many-many years, the marriage faltered anyway. I tried everything I could to overcome the issues she had with my children – and even I welcomed *her* two teenage children into our home, but that didn't really solve anything related to how she treated *my* kids.

Once again, I should have heeded the sign given to me: when I asked her how she would like it if I treated *her* kids the way she treated mine... she said, "I'd divorce you."

I was shocked at her answer and argued back to her that it wasn't fair to my kids and that I tried hard to get along with hers. She just shrugged her shoulders and said, "I'm not you."

I should have taken her advice right then, especially for my kids' sake, but I was stubborn. I wanted to figure out a way to make this marriage and our blended family work for all of us.

In the middle of December that year I went for a stress test as part of the follow-up to my stent surgery, and I failed the test. The doctor told me I needed to have heart bypass surgery and that I could either have it right away, or wait until after the Christmas-New Year holidays and take my chances of having a heart attack. I did not want to risk a heart attack, so I had open heart surgery and received a double-bypass on December 23, 1998. I was sent home just three days after my bypass surgery. I guess it was a combination of the Christmas holiday and my youth; I was only 45 years old when I had this operation.

The first night back home I had a terrible nightmare – with blood flowing everywhere. I woke up in a panic. My heart was racing. I thought I would die because my new bypasses were being so taxed. *The fast heartrate would surely make them explode and I would die instantly*, I thought. Of course, I didn't, but it sure was a scary feeling.

The second night I was home, I put on an angelic music CD next to my bed. I had trouble while I was going to sleep, and I was crying out to God to help me understand why He spared me. That night I had a vision – a dream-like scene appeared to me.

My Journey In The Shadow of "The King"
........From Graceland to the Promised Land

I saw what looked like a dozen angels floating above my bed. They were dancing around in a circle to the music on my music player. As I became more awake I was aware that it was about 3am – and I decided to lay perfectly still and just take all of this in. (Moving would surely cause a lot of pain and I didn't want to be distracted.) I had such a wonderful feeling of peace and joy. My body was no longer hurting from the surgery and I sensed a clear message being given to me. In essence it said, *"Everything is going to be okay. You will continue your music – but new music will be given to you and should be used to help others. It is not for you to make a profit or for you to get rich and famous."*

I was also told that, based on some of our previous marital discussions, my wife and I would definitely be moving and we would open a Bed & Breakfast that would help people "soothe their weary souls." I later decided to call the B&B *The Angel's Lair*. It was a great attention-getter for marketing and seemed fitting based on the experience I had. I even saw the layout of the third floor Victorian home that we ultimately purchased and renovated. It was an exhilarating experience - very inspiring and a spiritually healing one too.

It was during this recovery period that I saw a TV special on our cable network called *He Touched Me*. It was a documentary on Elvis' gospel roots and how he continued to sing gospel all during his career. He used to sing gospel all night long with his band members. He also sang gospel songs to warmup the backup singers before his concerts.

Elvis also followed Rex Humbard and his TV church services since he could not physically attend services. During the program, Elvis invited Rex and his wife backstage at one of his concerts in Vegas. They quoted the preacher's wife saying that, "Elvis was God's bell sheep" and that he would lead many people to Christ. This was *very* inspiring to me and confirmed to me that I could - and should - be doing more Elvis gospel singing. So I started putting together an all-gospel Elvis concert. I called it "The Other Side of Elvis" in order to help people realize how spiritual he was behind the scenes. His manager and record companies wanted to keep this from the public. They thought a gospel Elvis would ruin his Rock-n-Roll image.

At my wife's request and to fulfill her life-long dream of moving back home – hoping this could help our marriage and family issues - we moved to Bay City and we bought a run down 1880's Victorian mansion. We refurbished it and made it into the Bed & Breakfast I was told about in my vision. Believe it or not, I continued to work in the Detroit area – driving 86 miles each way – five days a week. This was necessary to maintain the income level needed to make all the house repairs and to fund the B&B. There were no jobs available in the Bay City area for my line of work that paid even half of the kind of money I was already making in the Detroit area.

All of this was a tremendous strain physically, emotionally, and financially. It took over three years to complete and two mortgages totaling over $360,000. Once it opened, the B&B took ALL of our time and I ultimately had to give up most of my singing – except for occasional Gospel Concerts when I was invited by a Pastor to appear at a church event. We went to several churches and did Elvis Gospel concerts. I did not wear a jumpsuit for these special concerts, instead I bought a black formal tuxedo with a white ruffled shirt with black stone cuff links surrounded by rhinestone diamonds. It was both conservative and a bit flashy with that Elvis flair.

My very first all-gospel Elvis concert was in my hometown of Bay City at a Lutheran church. They decided to give out free *tickets* in order to estimate seating capacity for the concert. God sure appeared to be in favor of this concert – they totally **sold out** all 400+ tickets within two hours of announcing the concert. I received a call the next day and they requested we book a second concert – which also came very close to selling out. It was an amazing feeling to sing songs to God in His "house." I was able to do several of these concerts while we were still in the renovation stage of the B&B. "The Other Side of Elvis" looked like it was a hit with local church audiences.

My Journey In The Shadow of "The King"
........From Graceland to the Promised Land

But inside of our own house and marriage, the stress was unrelenting and we were nearly divorced in early 2003. However, my second cousin who was the Head Pastor of his own Independent Christian Church (ICC) - where we also did a sell-out Elvis Gospel concert - asked me to see their *Christian* counselor Brian Jones for six weeks to bring Christ into our marriage and to work a miracle. Prior to that, all the counseling we attended had been secular, non-spiritual; but when Brian prayed over us and brought Christ into the midst – this time something was very different.

My Journey In The Shadow of "The King"
........From Graceland to the Promised Land

Something of a miracle did occur during this time. Shortly after starting the Christian counseling, I attended a Holy Spirit conference at ICC with Bob Sorge speaking – and during Bob's Friday night program, I received a message from GOD that He wanted me to quit trying to do things on my own, *"look what you have done with your life"* – *"have you had enough struggle?"* *"Come to me and I will give you rest"*.

That night, I gave my heart to Jesus – and fell face down on the ground at the altar and was washed in a BRIGHT light for some period of time. I immediately gave up vegetarianism and the Eastern Philosophy and began a renewed quest for Christian/Biblical knowledge and training.

I continued marriage counseling, but I had a new thirst for the knowledge of GOD's words – and I signed up for many training classes at the church. Through our local church, I ultimately became a student and graduate of the International School of Ministry (ISOM).

That year we were able to avert the divorce, but then something else occurred and the marriage never recovered. There was a tragic car accident in June 2003. My wife was nearly killed. She suffered a severe concussion and slurred speech for several days. She was never the same after that and became much worse and more violent than before about my kids and the music.

The sad thing was that during the 3-4 months following the accident, nobody from the church reached out to us during this troubled time. Later, during a Timothy Leadership Training class at church, when I confronted the church leaders, they challenged me right back. They said,

"Did you call us to tell us what happened?"

I confessed, no, I had not. I assumed that they would miss me at church and come looking for us, but they did not. With forgiveness in our hearts, we resumed our relationship with the church membership and continued attending services there.

The following September, the B&B opened and we ran it for nearly three years – again with quite a bit of stress and tension. I continued to drive 86 miles each way from Bay City to Auburn Hills 4-5 days a week to work in corporate America. I justified the hours on the road based on the pay I received which helped finance the renovations and B&B overhead. Things were going along fairly well until the Tech Stock bubble burst. My employer, Compuware, reduced my pay by 33% in late 2003. That caused even more stress to our situation.

My Journey In The Shadow of "The King"
........From Graceland to the Promised Land

In spite of all the resistance at home to my music, the Pastor at ICC helped pave the way for me to meet a Gospel Promoter so I could record a very professional – high-quality Elvis Gospel CD. Amazingly, whenever I performed an Elvis Gospel concert at a church, there were HUGE record-breaking crowds and many people were saved at several of my concerts. People were asking me for a CD of *me* singing the Gospel songs the way *I* was doing them at my concerts.

I wound up at the very studio where the TV documentary *He Touched Me* was recorded – Gaither Studios – owned by Bill Gaither. He wrote *He Touched Me*, one of the songs that Elvis received a Grammy award for. How awesome is that? A little orphan boy from Bay City, Michigan with a dream to be like Elvis, records a gospel CD at a major studio like that! What a blessing. Of course, we called the CD "The Other Side of Elvis" and it not only has *He Touched Me* on it, but we also included *How Great Thou Art* and my own special versions of _Amazing Grace_, *Love Me Tender Jesus,* and *The Wonder of You God* - along with many other Elvis gospel favorites that I performed at my Gospel concerts.

This was a bright light in my life. It was during this time that I felt a need to *give back* to the orphanage where I had been entertained years earlier by the band that shook my hand. So I went to St. Vincent's Home which had permanently moved to their Shields, MI location after their Saginaw location burned down due to a fire. I was eager to do a free Elvis concert for the kids, but I was surprised and disappointed by their answer to my offer. The manager informed me that they had changed their whole program and were no longer affiliated with the nuns at Daughters of Charity and the Knights of Columbus which helped fund the orphanage when I was there. They now only took in troubled boys from various life-threatening and dysfunctional family situations and they were certain that these boys would NOT be interested in an Elvis concert.

My Journey In The Shadow of "The King"
........From Graceland to the Promised Land

Once again, I was disappointed and I cried out to God, *"How can I give back when they refuse my offer?" "Help me find a way to give back to some needy children."* Then I remembered that I had passed by a home for boys many times in Bay City. The sign said it was a Lutheran Home and seemed like there might be a possibility that they would be interested in my offer – so I stopped by one day and met with Gordy, their onsite manager. Sure enough, Gordy was both interested and excited about my offer. But, there was a condition to his acceptance. The boys here were also from broken homes and abusive and neglected circumstances – they had to be sheltered from public recognition, so we had to be discrete about our activities. No pictures and no names of the boys were to be released. Since my sole goal was to help the boys (there were no girls at this facility because they had a separate housing site in another town for them) I quickly agreed with Gordy's terms.

My next challenge was what to do for the boys. Just doing a concert seemed like it was not enough. After talking with Gordy and his activity coordinator, Scott, we decided to do a Christmas concert for the boys and I had just the site in mind to host it: a local favorite of mine for both eating and doing my Elvis concerts – Krzysiak's Polish-American restaurant just up the road from the boys' home in Bay City. When I suggested the benefit concert to the owners Don and Lois they were immediately excited about it! They offered to cover dinner for ALL the boys and the staff. What an excellent start. But, I was still on a mission to make a major difference in these boys' lives, so I asked Gordy and Scott what else we could do for the boys besides just feed them and sing some Elvis Christmas songs. They said many of the boys had various needs for goods and toys/activities to keep them busy during their off-times. BINGO! A new goal was put into motion.

I had Scott interview each of the boys – I think there about 20+ of them – and I wanted to know, if they could have *anything* they wanted for Christmas, what would it be? I asked for at least 2-3 items per boy in case something was out of reach for my budget. (I really didn't have one yet – but I had more tricks up my sleeve for this special project.)

My Journey In The Shadow of "The King"
........From Graceland to the Promised Land

While Scott was getting ready to get his list started, I scheduled a time to stop by the home with my guitar and meet the boys and do a little impromptu mini-concert for them. They seemed a bit shy at first, but after a few songs, we exchanged some stories and I explained a little about the upcoming Christmas dinner concert – and that THEY were the guests of honor.

Then the real challenge began, I started reaching out to many of the businesses and influential friends I had made over the years thru all my singing and concerts in the area. We also told the concert attendees that they needed to bring a gift for a boy as part of their admission to the concert. Praise God, they all came through with donations of all kinds of things for the boys. Gordy had to haul the goods home in a pickup truck! (But, I'm getting ahead of myself!)

It was amazing to see the faces of the boys light up during their special dinner and the concert! Of course, I had to single out a few of the boys to get up on the dance floor (my stage area) during *Blue Suede Shoes* and help me do the Elvis dancing! They really got into it – and so did the crowd by encouraging them on. What a fun time we all had that night. Then to my surprise, when I did *Can't Help Falling* – Lois Krzysiak (the owner's wife) came forward and started pulling the boys one-by-one out of their seats and she danced with each of them. I still get choked up just thinking about how special that was!

Finally, at the end of the concert, I told the audience that we had a special treat for the boys and the staff brought out bags of toys. We started calling names, one at a time and we watched the boys open their gifts from the list Scott had created. There was not a dry eye in the place and the boys became even more ecstatic over their new treasures! I found out later that some of them went home and cried all night about getting a toy they had wanted for years.

That first year was so successful that we wound up doing it again over the next couple of years. Ultimately the donations increased to the point where we literally got every boy EVERYTHING that was on their list. The last year that we did it, we also provided the home itself with many extra items for ALL the boys to use, like basketball hoops, balls, board games and other items for activity times.

I think it was around the second year of doing these benefit concerts and on-site mini-concerts for the boys, Gordy called me and said one of the boys asked him to relay a question to me:

"Why does this guy care about us? He doesn't even know us."

A lump formed in my throat as I answered Gordy, "You go tell that young man that when I was his age, I was also in an orphanage, and people came and did things for us. Now that I am an adult, it's MY turn to do something for you; and when you grow up it will be your turn."

What an awesome opportunity. I thanked God for His goodness and that I was able to return it to someone in need.

After the third year of doing these annual benefits for the Lutheran Boys Home, Gordy approached me and said his host organization, the *Lutheran Child & Family Service* of Michigan, was hosting their annual statewide conference in Frankenmuth, Michigan. He wanted me to attend so they could recognize me and my efforts to help the boys. I told him it wasn't just me that did all of these things; there were many helpers along the way. He said he was aware of all the other helpers, but he knew the whole thing started with my drive to help the boys. I repeated that recognition was not necessary, just seeing the expressions on the boys' faces was more than enough for me. But, Gordy was insistent and he also asked me to make a speech.

"A speech? About what?" I exclaimed.

He said **"Danny, your story is very encouraging to the boys and to our staff and counselors alike. We will have staff members and counselors from all over Michigan, and they need to hear your story of coming from a broken home, to an orphanage, and then into music and a successful corporate career. Your story needs to be heard."**

THIS WAS AN AMAZING WAKE-UP CALL TO ME.

I did the speech and received their recognition certificate and filed it away – until several years later when Gordy's words kept coming back to me.

Figure 7: Gordy and me 2004
Figure 8: Recognition Certificate 2005

Ultimately – **this is why you are able to read this book right now**.

It has been my dream to share with others who are struggling to make it through their challenges in life; that, if one keeps a strong focus on moving forward, and an even stronger faith in God – you can walk through the storms in life and emerge even better than you were before. YOU ARE NOT ALONE! God is with you. So, let Him work with you and try always to get BETTER – not BITTER - when you go through life's challenges.

Even though we were having some fun and successes through my musical escapades, my wife continued her resistance to *any* music that I wanted to do. But, deep down in my heart, I knew that this is why God made me. I had no other feeling in the world like I did when I was singing on stage (especially for GOD!).

Stressed to the max - Christ takes center stage

In the spring of 2007, my wife announced she no longer wanted to do the Bed & Breakfast. I was on my own. Eventually she started resisting even having guests in our home. What was I going to do now? The B&B was supposed to pay for itself – and help pay down the debt! We were just starting to make a profit and I could see us paying off the debt within five years. But NOT without the B&B income.

Now I was even MORE stressed over this latest development. How was I supposed to manage a B&B business on my own while maintaining a daytime job over 80 miles away? Many phone calls would come in throughout the day, and for a while I attempted to cover them from work by taking intermittent "breaks" as needed. Of course, after a while my boss caught on to my frequent bathroom breaks and sudden disappearances. When I confessed to her what was going on, she told me she understood, and because my work was always up-to-date, she personally did not have a problem with my way of handling my home issues. She told me to just be careful about how often I was talking on the phone to my wife and others because other people in the work unit could overhear my conversations. I felt very overwhelmed and at a loss for what to do. Once again I prayed to God for help and insight about how to handle all of these stressful events.

My Journey In The Shadow of "The King"
........From Graceland to the Promised Land

Be careful what you pray for, because God has His own way of working things out. I abruptly lost my job in August 2007 and eventually wound up filing for bankruptcy. I was out of work over four months during the financial bubble when jobs in Michigan were scarce. During that down time, I made an extensive Bible study of suffering - especially in the book of Job. I prayed for Wisdom to know what GOD wanted me to do. I was growing VERY weary of pushing so hard all the time. For years my life had been *full* of stress both at work and at home. My favorite way to reduce stress – singing – was off limits because my wife threatened to divorce me if I didn't give up singing completely. So I decided to *stay down* and allow God to open the doors when *He* was ready for me to move on.

It was during this time that I was inspired to write some more new songs. I had an inspiration one night – God kept telling me, "*It's okay, you are not alone, I am with you.*" Sound familiar? It was His theme for the Angel song – *I Hear an Angel Whispering*. This time, I was inspired to write about being held in God's arms – and *In His Arms* was born. **"In His arms are all my answers, In His arms I will find peace. His loving arms – are all I really need."** It was so inspirational and very much needed during this major trial of financial failure and bankruptcy.

There is an old saying – "let go and let God." Well that is exactly what was happening to me at this time in my life. I was used to *making* things happen. I would make calls - and things would get done. If they moved too slowly, I made more calls and kept calling on others until I got my way! Well, this time, it was different. I learned that GOD is in control – not me. It is when we become humble that God can finally do His best work in us.

With the B&B closed and little income coming in, I was receiving unemployment insurance payments from the State of Michigan. We wound up selling off our assets, including all the antiques we had purchased for the B&B, and decided to let the house go back to the bank. The bankruptcy also cleared the second mortgage and all the other debts. This actually became a GREAT relief for me – I was out of debt!

But for now, we were in limbo with a very depressing cloud of shame hanging over us during the whole bankruptcy process. I had always paid my own bills and was very-very depressed about being a failure. In my Bible studies, I discovered a Biblical precedent for partaking in the bankruptcy process based on Romans chapter 13. Even though our society doesn't follow all of God's laws, it gave me some consolation that He expects us to follow the laws of our government. Bankruptcy is one-such law that offered financial protection under the circumstances I was in. In the Old Testament instructions for Israel, God also provided a 7-year debt cancellation provision; (it's in Deuteronomy 15 verses 1-2) and that gave me some consolation to know God's heart on the matter. Amazingly, it had been seven years since we bought the Victorian house and took out the first loan. I was crushed with the thought of not paying back my debts. It was devastating to me – so this Bible study and God's answers were very helpful and timely for me.

Finally, in January 2008 I got a job offer, but it was in Ohio for an IT company called CareTech. It was a FRESH start, but we had to move. This wound up being another blessing because the bank had not yet started the eviction process. Now that we were moving, we could just vacate the house and turn the keys over to the bank. In the end, it was a better way for us to deal with that transition.

Since we were moving out of state, I was not able to complete my ISOM studies at the ICC church, but that was NOT going to be the end of that training. I was able to pick it up again later as an online class. I *really* wanted to complete this training and achieve my Associate's degree in Theology which came with completion of the course.

Ultimately, the move to Cincinnati was the beginning of the end for the marriage. My wife *hated* Ohio and was *very* depressed and angry with me for *dragging* her there. She complained every day and threatened to leave me and move back to Michigan by Christmas if I didn't get a transfer or get a job in Michigan by then. After a few months things also became even tenser at work, because I got a new boss and he was badgering me even worse than I was getting at home. He even tried to get me fired.

To make a long-story short – my wife left me in December 2008. It happened when I took a weekend trip by myself and went home to Bay City to visit family. While she was moving out that weekend, she trashed all my entertainment items into six dumpsters at a strip mall around the corner from our Ohio apartment. That was the final straw for me and we wound up separated from December 2008 until the divorce was final in March of 2010.

All during the time that I was in Ohio, I continued to pursue God and longed to worship musically and learn MORE about Him and His ways. I studied at church and under a former Jewish minister, Pastor James H, as well as Perry Stone, Shane Willard, and online with the International School of Ministry (ISOM). I was also counseled by Pastor Carl P and Pastor Brad W via phone calls and periodic visits back to Michigan.

Then the call came in June 2009 to move my job with CareTech back to Michigan.

At my wife's request, I tried once more during that time to put the marriage back together, but that only lasted for 8-9 weeks. I had to move away from her for good when she took a hammer after my remaining things and threatened me saying, "Somebody will get hurt if you stay here." Then she called the police. They arrived and stayed onsite while I moved my things out of the apartment. I finally had enough and filed for divorce in September 2009. (It was final in March 2010).

Following this was a time of great spiritual development for me. After I moved back to Michigan, while visiting my mother in Bay City, I attended Fountain Ministries Church with Pastor Brad W. I met and studied with Pastor Jamie P. I went on several retreats with him to Holy Spirit and other conferences. My favorite was the *Via de Cristo* (Way of Christ) men's weekend where Christian men (Chachos) surround weekend candidates and are spiritually, physically, and prayerfully treated just like Christ did for those around Him. There were many lessons and living examples of REAL Godly love in action. There was also a lot of prayer, classes, music, food, and fellowship! This weekend led me to volunteer for a prison ministry where I actually performed *Jailhouse Rock* inside of a jail! (Yes, the warden danced too!) It was awesome!

I also re-connected with long-time friend and singing Pastor Tom D - who continues to be the embodiment of faith like no one I have ever met.

There was much to be learned and demonstrated regarding how powerful faith was to those who are willing to focus on God. During this time, I saw many wonderful things in Christ – including people being healed and overcome by the JOY of the Holy Spirit – right before my eyes! I, myself, was healed of arthritis...and to this day it has never returned. It was a wonderful and spiritually fulfilling time.

Be Wise!

YOU REALLY DO BECOME LIKE THE PEOPLE YOU HANG OUT WITH!

HE WHO WALKS WITH WISE MEN WILL BE WISE,

BUT THE COMPANION OF FOOLS WILL BE DESTROYED.

PROVERBS 13:30

My Journey In The Shadow of "The King"
........From Graceland to the Promised Land

Then in January 2010, one of my corporate bosses at CareTech (who was a distant relative) asked me if I had contacted any of our Italian relatives since I got back to Michigan. When I said no, he suggested that I really should. (It was like God directed this chance encounter.)

I *immediately* thought of my distant cousin – the one who let me stay with her and her husband back in the 70's. About a week or two later I finally found her phone number and called her. She was excited to hear from me and we arranged a time for me to stop by and visit the family; of course, I brought my guitar. It was at that gathering at her house that I met Lena K. This was the beginning of a *new* and fresh start for me (and Lena). God is GOOD!

Lena was very different from most women I encountered. She was very genuine and sincere. I could talk to her like nobody else. While I was consoling her and helping her through her own trials in life, she also had a way of comforting my spirit. I felt very much at peace around Lena, both on the phone and in person. While I knew in my mind that I needed time to heal from my recent divorce, my heart was telling me that Lena was VERY special and that I needed to stay close to her. I struggled with this for several months, but in the end, my heart, and Lena's overwhelming love, won! Then,

one night she asked me **to dance**.....

My Journey In The Shadow of "The King"
........From Graceland to the Promised Land

.....and Lena and I are truly living HAPPILY ever-after!

What a great and gracious God we have to ultimately give us the desires of our heart. All I really wanted in a partner for life has come true for me in Lena. We got married in October 2010. Since we have been together, the peace that I had been begging for has materialized even beyond my dreams. We have common goals, both spiritual and family focused. She loves my music and shares my successes and comforts me in my trials. As we began our lives together, we were both so overjoyed to be sharing everything life had for us; good and bad. We knew that together, with God at the helm, we could overcome anything.

Enchanted

I was so joyful about this new lifestyle with Lena that I just *had* to write her a song about it. I woke up one night, just before Valentine's Day, and was inspired to write the song *Enchanted*. The heart of the song goes like this...

As we praise God together, and read His holy Word,
I love the life that we're living, and the laughter thatis heard.
And, I'm enchanted...
Your Love has moved me to this mountain – of Joy and Ecstasy,
And we're connected at a level – that was just a Dream to me...
Now I'm Enchanted - My world is so Enchanted –
Ever since you've come along...
So Enchanted – It's like Agape Love.

Well, you get the gist of the internal joy and peace I have discovered through God's grace. But this was just the beginning of what God had in store for us! When I shared the new song with the various pastors I was visiting, they were *all* impressed and suggested the song be used for marriage encounters and counseling. One of them said, "It's the way God intends marriage to be."

As enchanted as my life had become, there was still an element of stress waiting around the corner. But this time, I had some loving support to help me get through it.

Two weeks after we got married, my project at CareTech came to a point where they decided they didn't need me anymore. That's right, downsized again! The economy in Michigan had not really recovered yet and it took me a full year to get another job. But what a difference a day makes! Lena was so supportive that we decided to focus on my music and a new small business was formed. She became my personal manager and we started performing Elvis mini-concerts for Senior Homes all around the area. I had already retired from my original Rock-n-roll Elvis shows and the Elvis Gospel never really took off the way we expected due to *Religious* objections from some conservative church members and leaders. I revamped my show for the seniors (many of whom were the original Elvis fans anyway) and I combined the lighter-cleaner Rock-n-Roll songs with some Elvis Gospel and was able to bring God into every concert we did. The seniors loved it! I even added some of my originals when time permitted. Once again, *I Hear an Angel Whispering* emerged as a crowd favorite.

While all this was unfolding, I continued with my Bible studies and discovered another Old Testament instruction that God gave the Hebrews for newlyweds. It commanded that after a couple got married, the man was not allowed to work or go to war for one year. He was to stay home and bring happiness to his wife. You can find this in Deuteronomy, chapter 24 verse 5. Now, I know we are not saved by keeping Old Testament laws, and I did not intentionally lose my job; in fact, until I had time to study the Bible more closely about these things, I never even heard of such a thing as staying home for a year! But there it is. Even though I tried to get another job, it was literally a full year, October 2011, before I landed a new corporate position.

To me, it shows that even when we don't consciously push to do things God's way, He sets things up for us.

It turned out to be a fabulous year for learning more about Lena and doing things together that we both loved. We formed an incredible bond and implicit trust for each other during this time.

Ordained Minister – New Music

Since I was also determined to complete my spiritual training via the online ISOM course, this extra time-off from corporate distractions allowed me the extra time I needed. I finally received my Associates Degree in Theology in 2011. Then I was able to become an ordained minister in 2012. The plan was to validate my Elvis Gospel show by demonstrating that I was a man focused on God and not portraying the bad-boy image that Elvis had shown to the general public. Most people don't know that Elvis only received *three* Grammys in his entire career; and all three were for his Gospel music. His first was for *How Great Thou Art* in 1967, then for *He Touched Me* in 1972, and finally for his *concert version* of *How Great Thou Art* in 1974. Of course, I performed all of these and more for my Gospel concerts.

All the while, Lena and I were traveling together around Michigan as I performed my Elvis shows and Elvis Gospel concerts. It was great to have such comforting support and be surrounded by such joy and peace.

This new lifestyle allowed me to open up more to God, and as I did, He opened up more to me. As I continued my fervent studies I began to *hear* more and more music and I started writing and singing even more new songs. Some of the new titles He gave me are:

> **One** – the story of Adam's rib becoming Eve and how marriage
> re-joined them into ONE....
> *"One-then-two-then-one…that's how it all begun"*.

My Journey In The Shadow of "The King"
........From Graceland to the Promised Land

All My Burdens – "_I give my burdens to You – Jesus....You can handle them all_".

Be Healed - as I myself was being healed from my past burdens, I was inspired to do a Bible study on healing. This song is composed entirely of direct Bible Scriptures; _every line_ is directly from the Bible.

Peace – I just couldn't help but write about the peace I was experiencing.

"_....There is Peace everywhere – there is Peace all around....There is Love in the air.....where You are found_". (A testimony to the presence of God and His Holy Spirit.) I am so grateful to have finally found it!

Feel the Joy! – As I was studying about God's promises and the healing that He has for us, I discovered the verse that says "_Eye has not seen, nor ear heard, nor has it entered into the mind of man the things that God has prepared for him._" (1 Cor 2:9) And also that when He returns, "_when He is revealed, we shall be like Him (Jesus)_". That's in 1 John 3:2.

WOW!....People, did you get that? God plans to transform us all to become just like Jesus! We will ALL be like Him in every way. When I finally understood that, I was _OVERJOYED_ with incredible excitement about being included in God's Kingdom with Jesus as my friend (and brother). This song quickly became one of Lena's favorites. She especially likes the studio music version where my friend Noel pays the piano solo! Praise God – He is so good to us!!! No wonder the angels shout for joy!!!

There are many more new songs, and there are also more adventures that Lena and I have been sharing since we got married.

To hear the songs above:
go to <u>www.broadjam.com/songs/DannyVann</u> or if in eBook, click the link

As we were cruising along in our new joy-filled life, we travelled around Michigan while I was doing periodic concerts for both secular and Gospel settings. The year after we were married I was booked for an Elvis concert at a major outdoor amphitheater in Clio, Michigan. The seating capacity there was over 2,500 and we nearly had a sellout! Lena's daughter from Florida was visiting with her family that week and decided to come to the concert.   Lena's other daughter, who lives about two miles from our house, also decided to attend. This would be the first time most of them had seen me perform in concert. What an exciting time for ALL of us! To make things more interesting, I called two of the Florida grandkids up on stage during the show. Like I had done so many times before, I had the kids dance with me during one of the songs. Both the kids, and the audience had a great time during this staged and shortened version of Jailhouse Rock!!!

Just before the end of the concert, there were some dark thunderhead clouds off in the distance, and it looked like a storm might bring the concert to an abrupt end. Then something amazing happened! As I began to sing my last song, *How Great Thou Art* – the sun peeped out and a beautiful rainbow formed high in the sky behind the backs of the audience. The band and I could see it quite clearly…..so I pointed and told the audience to look at what God was doing during His song! You could hear the oooooo's and ahhhhh's all over the amphitheater grounds. What an incredible end to an amazing concert.

As usual, after the show I met with audience members at a souvenir table that Lena and her daughters were tending for me. The rainbow was *still* visible and we were able to take some pictures of me and others (audience and family members) with the rainbow in the background. Several years later, people were still talking about that day and the sign from the heavens. It never did rain on us during or after the concert, but it rained all around us.

I continued doing small private shows from time to time and had gained some weight over the past few years and it was taking its toll on my ability to be as active on stage as I was once was in my earlier years. I told myself that my age certainly had nothing to do with it, although I knew the older I got, eventually I would have to give up all the dancing that had become part of my *normal* Rock-n-roll concerts. It was during this time that I realized that I really preferred to be doing Gospel concerts anyway, and that I should stop taking those Rock-n-roll types of bookings. At the same time I also noticed that the audiences were much more aggressive than they were back in the 70's and 80's. Lena and I agreed that I needed to modify my show to fit my new focus. I also felt awkward with those old dance moves since I had become an ordained minister. It just didn't seem right to me anymore.

My major focus during the early days of our marriage was on my daytime job which kept me quite busy. Since the time I came into Lena's life and we began to be so active in the community, her daughter's family in Florida started begging us to make a trip to see them down there. Both Lena and I also wanted to eventually travel to visit all of our outstate kids. (My two kids were raising their families in Arizona and Virginia.) So, after many weeks of discussions and mental preparation, Lena finally agreed to buy her first-ever plane ticket and to fly to Florida! It took me explaining that God has us all *In His Arms*, and that she should picture herself sitting in her airplane seat as God had her cradled in His arms – with her head resting on His chest. We finally made the trip with her son Christopher. We all had a fabulous vacation with the family. It was a great bonding experience for everyone.

When we got back to Michigan from our Florida vacation, I performed what would be my *last* Rock-n-Roll concert for a private group back in Clio, Michigan. I remember struggling to get through a couple of the more active songs like Viva Las Vega and Suspicious Minds. They were traditionally longer, high-energy, sing-and-dance songs for me. Even though I toned down the dancing, I just couldn't help being hyperactive during those songs.

Imagine trying to sing full force as you did a high-energy aerobic workout. Well, I made it through the show, but I sensed something was off. I just chalked it up to being out of shape from doing so few shows lately.

In the meantime, the new job in corporate America I had was changing from when I first signed on two years earlier. I had already been moved to three different bosses, and the one that originally agreed to my working terms was no longer in the picture. My *newest* boss was very excited about my skills and abilities and wanted to make me the senior leader over his new high-cost, high-profile project. This was something that I knew I did *not* want to do because my heart-health issues had been getting worse as I grew older. Those stress-filled days at the office were beginning to take their toll on me and my cardiologist warned me to reduce stress.

Then it happened.....

In March 2013, we had an important project meeting and I needed to present the overall plan for the big project. I was feeling *off* again, but this time something was different. I was very-very tired and had low energy. I told my boss that I was going to go to my car to rest over lunch, just before the meeting, and that I would be back to start the meeting on time. Then I called Lena and she suggested that I come home if I didn't feel well. I explained how important the meeting was and assured her I would be okay of I just took a brief nap. (Go figure – the meeting and work were more important to me than my health at that moment in time.) So, after my nap, I went back into my office and started the meeting, but my energy quickly drained again and I wound up leaving the meeting early and driving myself back home. It was about a 40 minute drive.

When I got home, Lena took one look at me and said I needed to go to the ER. I shrugged it off and said all I needed was a nap. She insisted I go to ER and called my Mom who lived up in Bay City, but I kept repeating that I was okay and all I needed was some rest. Lena continued to persist – I needed to go to the ER and I needed to go now! She could see something was wrong with me. Finally, after Lena called my sister, I agreed to humor them and go to the local Urgent Care clinic a mile from our home. When they took my vital signs, the doctor came back in and said they called an ambulance for me, it appeared that I was having a heart attack! WHAT? What a shock that was to me! They immediately gave me four baby aspirins - I knew then that this was a serious issue.

At the ER, after treating me with blood thinners, taking many more blood samples and running other tests, the ER doctor came in and told me that I was lucky that I came in when I did. I just had a pretty significant heart attack. He explained that if I had taken a nap, as I wanted to do, that I would never have awakened! God spared me again and Lena helped save my LIFE! Now the strength of our marriage and relationship were really going to be tested.

That day I received my first heart catherization (cath) and they placed a stent in what I found out later was my widow-maker artery. The next day, I got another heart cath this time through my wrist and I received two more stents. My cardiologist proclaimed me permanently disabled. He said my arteries were a mess and that I was in the advanced stages of arteriosclerosis. This actually was not a big surprise to me, I had been treated for over 30 years for high cholesterol and the doctors told me this day would come. I just didn't expect it to come when it did. But, then again, who does?

My medical "Exodus" – Family support

The next few months were very foggy for me – it was almost like living through a dream. There were so many changes that I had to make, both in actions and thoughts. I was now homebound, and for weeks Lena had to drive me to my rehab sessions where my progress was quite slow by my standards. I took all the free classes they offered so I could get educated on how to avoid a repeat heart attack – or worse. Lena was a trooper, she even attended some of the classes with me. Her loving support and care of me was incredible. God certainly blessed me with the perfect mate for this time in my life. We had to make many adjustments to our lifestyle as we worked through my rehabilitation.

My Journey In The Shadow of "The King"
........From Graceland to the Promised Land

Then came the financial changes, I lost 80% of my income for the short-term disability period. All the while medical bills started arriving in our mailbox. It was not exactly the best way for a heart attack victim to start a *stress-free* life. But, through it all we kept our faith in God and trusted He would help us through – and He DID! Yes, we drained our savings to cover our expenses, but that's what they were there for anyway. Except it was a terrible feeling to now be without that financial cushion. About the time we cashed in our last 401K the long-term benefits kicked in and my income was restored to 70% of my original salary....and because it was disability income it was *tax free*! Finally things were looking up for us financially. Although it would take many-many months to pay off all the medical bills. But, there was still my long road to physical recovery; and even then it was not a complete 100% recovery.

It took months to regain even 50% of my strength and stamina. My cardiologist reported that I lost 30% of my heart function and that my arteries were a mess.

Around August of that year I was taking short walks around our subdivision and on my way back home I suddenly felt anxious – my heart seemed to be racing – and it did not stop. So about 1 ½ blocks from home I sat on a park bench on the walking path and monitored my heart beat. I was sure it would calm down if I sat and rested...wrong again! So, I got up and walked very slowly the rest of the way home. Lena was out running errands so I called her and she rushed home and called 911. They took me to the ER again, and I discovered that I was in Afib – a heart issue where the top half and bottom half of the heart are beating out of sync. It is pretty serious and can lead to blood clots, stroke and yes, even another heart attack – and death. So, they admitted me and kept me overnight to see if my heart would revert back to normal rhythm on its own. It didn't, so I was taken back into the operating room for another heart cath and they found another new blockage and I got another stent. The Afib did not correct itself, so they also used the paddles and shocked my heart back into its proper rhythm. Now of course, I was taking a few steps backward – and they added more drugs to my long list of necessary meds to help stabilize my condition and keep my heart from beating too hard or too fast.

All this caused me to be in such a fog that I did not even pick up my guitar for months.....both music and my life were on hold. I couldn't help but be depressed about all of these things happening. But, I knew God was still there directing it all. I just didn't know where it was all leading me. I began to feel like one of the children of Israel when they were walking through the desert of the exodus from Egypt. I was just wandering through life daily, always tired and always groggy with no real sense of direction or purpose. I was just trudging along day-by-day. It took nearly two years for me to begin to come out of the fog from it all.

I was grateful to God for sparing me, but for what? What purpose did all this mean for me and my wife and family? What was I supposed to do now? I dug deeper into my bible studies and began to see what Solomon – the wisest man in the world - meant when he wrote Ecclesiastes – all of this is vanity (delusion) – we cannot control our circumstances, we can only react to them. And the more we depend on God and have faith in His ways, the better our reactions will be for us.

God gives wisdom to those who ask for it. I had asked for that wisdom years earlier, and it was slowly being dished out to me. Looking back now, I can see how God spoon-fed me only as much as I could tolerate (although at times I felt like I was at my breaking point). Unfortunately, it seems I learned much more through the disasters in my life than from the good times. What about you? Think about it, what motivates you the most to make changes in your life? Is it those painful situations, or do you seek better ways of doing things during the good moments? For me, pain has been quite an effective motivator.

At one point I felt like I was in prison – the four walls of my living room were my confinement cell. I cried out to God, *"Why am I here? How can I serve you and others if I can't even leave my house?"*. I talked to my pastor about it and he led me into more bible studies about how God can use us in all circumstances. Then it occurred to me that the apostle Paul wrote four of his epistles (letters) - to the Ephesians, Philippians, Colossians and Philemon -from PRISON! He even called himself Christ's bondservant. This perspective gave me new hope that I could still be useful to God even from my living room "cell".

When I shared this perspective with our church pastor, he agreed and encouraged me to keep moving forward with my studies. We also discussed using some of the new music God gave me to minister to others via *care* packages with a CD and cover letter. I would use the music and a personal letter with Scripture references to help other church members through their own trials and circumstances. The pastor would work closely with me at first to help guide my words and mailings and over time Lena and I would make the decisions on who and when to send a package to.

Never give up!

Today, five years after my heart attack, nine total heart caths and seven stents; as I write this, I want to encourage you to never give up. Never stop reaching out to God and your fellow man for answers and the hope of God which He gave us through His son Jesus Christ. Don't just get angry and quit! That solves nothing. If you have given up on God, take a step back and review your past and see if you can tell where He really was there for you all along. Maybe your anger and resentment just got in the way of seeing what He was doing for you. Many times, even the worst of things that happen to us can be turned around into a benefit for not only ourselves, but it can also provide a way to help someone else go through a similar event.

At the end of the Exodus, in the book of Deuteronomy, after 40 years of wandering in the desert, the Israelites did inherit the Promised Land. In spite of all they went through to get there – God came through and made good on His promise. He is ready to do that for each of us, but we cannot quit. We need to keep going, keep moving forward.

My Journey In The Shadow of "The King"
........From Graceland to the Promised Land

When I started documenting the events in my life in order to help others who are at a place I once came through, I was hoping to be able to make a difference for others – now I can also see, to a greater extent, that God has allowed me to work through more of my own issues and become even more grateful for ALL that He has done for me. My prayer for you is that you can also let go of your pain and reflect on your life in a way that will be helpful to you and your family and friends….and embrace it all with a new perspective.

It has been a challenging journey, and I am a long way from my original starting point of wanting to be just like Elvis and get my own Graceland….but, through it all I have grown into my own person in both body and spirit and I have found an even better person to imitate – Jesus Christ. His reward is the Promised Land of Paradise. I'm still here, so He isn't done with me yet; and I now look forward to the coming adventures (and lessons) that He has in store for me and my family. In the meantime, I encourage you to keep walking in faith and hope, that you may also find this peace and joy for yourself!

My Journey In The Shadow of "The King"
........From Graceland to the Promised Land

NOTE: There are many events documented in this book that may appear shocking to some readers. Please know that the key to moving forward in life is *FORGIVENESS*! I have forgiven my parents and everyone that has offended me. As Christ has forgiven me, I have forgiven others to the fullest extent that I am able. Christ told us to do that in Matthew 6:14 – both in the Lord's Prayer and in several other places in the New Testament – like Matthew 18:22 and Mark 11:25-26. I have spent many years examining, questioning and trying to understand why certain things happened to me and my siblings during our lives. I'm sure many of you have done the same for tragic events in your lives. One thing that I have learned is that: HURTING PEOPLE USUALLY HURT OTHER PEOPLE. That is to say, when someone hurts you, then you are more likely not going to trust others and if someone does something similar to you – you will probably strike out – and hurt them like you were hurt.

Now I'm not saying that everyone will do that. Some people will do the opposite. When they see how much pain was inflicted on them, they will recognize what a terrible thing that has happened so they will make extra sure that they do NOT do something like that to others. In my family's case, there were hurt parents, who were *very* young when they found themselves with children. They reacted to life's events and did what their instincts told them as things progressively got worse and worse.

There were times when I was angry. There were times when I wanted to get revenge or to retaliate in some way. There were even times when I totally cut off communication with each of my parents. ***NONE of these actions changed anything that happened to me.*** I began to realize that my parents are people too. Like me, they made mistakes and they decided to do some things for the wrong reasons or at the wrong times. But, I have found out that in their heart of hearts, they did the best they could at the time. None of us can BE, or actually live inside of another person. We can never know precisely what anyone was thinking at any time in the past (even if that person tries to tell us at a later date – they themselves cannot explain with 100% recall *EVERYTHING* that was going on in their mind and heart when they decided to do something).

Throughout the years, I have learned many things about my parents, and other relatives that helped me understand and explain how *they* were brought up – or what they were taught – or what the culture of the day was at the time of the event. When some things were revealed, it was like a curtain was raised on that stage of my life and my heart leaped for joy. A huge burden was lifted – and compassion and forgiveness took center stage! I was able to cry about the pain and let it go once and for all.

For example, it troubled all of us kids for many years that a Mom could give up her six children and move out of town. Why did our Mom leave us at St. Vincent's Home? One day when I was reminiscing with one of our cousins who used to be our babysitter, the subject of mom's escapades came up and Bernie told me the origin of mom's solution to the problem of not being able to earn enough money and still manage six kids at home as a single parent. Bernie told us that when Mom was young, her mother (Grandma Josie) also struggled with managing and feeding eight kids and two adults on Grandpa's fruit-truck vendor earnings during the Great Depression. (My mom and dad were BOTH born during the Depression – and they were the younger siblings of large families. They both grew up in the Depression-era and during World War II.) Apparently, back in the old country, it was no big deal for Sicilian families to help with the burdens of other family members by taking in some of each other's children until the parents could get back on their feet. Grandma Josie's brother, Uncle Cecil, lived next door to grandma's house with his wife, Aunt Marion. And Aunt Marion just loved my mom. So when times got tough, Mom moved into Uncle Cecil and Aunt Marion's house. While there, she was spoiled and doted on (like Grandma did with me).

Later in mom's life, when she was an adult with a large family that she couldn't feed and clothe, she also sent us out to some of her relatives. But after a time, they eventually needed to send us back home to Mom before she could get back on her feet financially. She struggled for quite a while with us and it was a natural jump for her to seek a way to keep us together and still get much needed help. So she went to the Catholic Family Services and they agreed that putting us temporarily into the St. Vincent's Home would be best for all of us. This insight was like a bright light to my understanding of why our lives changed so drastically on that fateful day we were dropped off at the Home.

Understanding took the place of darkness; anger and pain dissolved like a lump of dirt in the rain. I have learned that *HATE* is a **poison** inside of our bodies. It spawns terrible chemical reactions and usually drives the hater to actually become just like the person they hate. It has been said that unforgiveness is like taking poison and then waiting for the *other* person to die. How crazy is that?

If you harbor any anger or hate (in *any* form) I would encourage you to take a step back from your pain and look to see the evil doer from another perspective. Why did they think this was a good thing to do? (Obviously good for *them*, not necessarily for *you*.) What could have happened in their life that taught them to do something like they did? If you were a child when the event happened, try to understand that. Now that you are an adult, you need to let go of your child-like feelings that you have held onto since you were wronged. Re-examine the situation through the eyes of your ADULT personality. Yes, it will hurt to relive the experience, but let's be honest, you probably have been replaying the scene in your mind since it happened anyway.

What I am suggesting is that you replay it from the *adult* perspective. See the tragedy of it all – be appalled and angry with the person causing the pain. But, do it as an adult. Imagine what the *child* should be experiencing and recognize the whole picture unfolding. Then LET IT GO! Stop carrying it with you. Verbally confess "I FORGIVE __so-and-so_____" – SAY THE WHOLE PHRASE – WITH THEIR NAME - OUT LOUD! Mean it when you confess it. And whenever the thoughts come back – and they will, THEN – SAY IT AGAIN – "I FORGIVE _____."

It is a conscious decision to forgive. You may never completely forget the situation, but, gradually you'll begin to let go of the freshness of the pain and anger. You will begin to feel relief and sympathy for the "child" that was wronged. You will let go of the need for revenge or retribution. You won't want the other person to do anything to make up for it anymore. It will finally be over! The whole event will look like a movie screen and you will be able to discuss it without emotion. Vengeance is mine says the LORD! (Romans 12:19, Deut. 32:35.) If you believe in God, then you must believe His words and His promises. Know that someday justice will prevail, but not always *our* way or at the time we think it should be done. In the end – it is "His Will" that will be done! Jesus reminded us that *"not one sparrow falls to the ground without His order. You are worth much more than many sparrows.....even the hairs on your head are numbered."*

When our God pays that much attention to the details, you can see that He is in *total and complete control* of everything that happens. When someone's free will interferes with our life, He will right the wrong and ultimately see that they receive the *reward* (or *punishment*) for their actions. But, we must learn to trust Him and leave the results in His hands. I know it is easier said than done, but, once we have pursued the common/legal options to deal with a problem, then we need to leave the remainder in our Heavenly Father's capable hands. That is when and where we finally get REST for our spirit; when we give it all to Him. I saw a night shirt at a gift shop that said "When you go to sleep at night, give your problems to God. He's up all night anyway." It's a little light humor, but very truthful. God is always watching over us and He wants to help us – if we would just let go of trying to do everything ourselves. So, let go – and let God!

My Journey In The Shadow of "The King"
........From Graceland to the Promised Land

When you're a young child, it's natural to want to please your parents and in most cases want to be like either your Mom or your dad. Well I spent most of my life wanting to be like Elvis! I mean I watched EVERY movie at the theaters and on TV (this was before videos and DVDs were available). I listened to every record and album I could get my hands on – over-and-over-and-over again. I learned how he breathed. I learned every inflection, every pause, hesitation and guttural slur that he did so effortlessly. But in spite of all the "study" and practice I put in to become more like Elvis – do you know what emerged as I got older? I learned that I had also been *imitating* somebody else in my daily activities.....not my dad....not my mom...I was imitating all the things I had been taught about Christ Jesus. At one time, I had memorized the Ten Commandments and I guess they took hold in my heart because I had no interest in doing things that went against them.

Another thing I guess you could say encouraged me to be like Christ was that Elvis put on a persona in his early career as an all American clean cut boy with a church background. As a budding teen when Elvis hit his height, the stories of his generosity and children's benefits impressed me a lot. I too did a LOT of benefit concerts. Sometimes my managers used them for ulterior motives like exposure and TV/radio coverage. But, I was always ready, willing, and by the grace of God, able to help people less fortunate than me. Trust me, I knew what it was like to be poor or have your home taken away from you at a moment's notice.

It's one thing to "talk" about people who need a helping hand – or to just drop some coins in a collection basket or Salvation Army bucket, but to actually meet the people that have the need - - - well that makes things a lot more personal and meaningful. It is said that when you are feeling down, go find someone worse off and help *them*. Abe Lincoln said "To ease another's heartache is to forget one's own." Somehow I just wanted to help everyone that I possibly could - whenever I could. So I did benefit concerts for burned-out families who lost their home, cancer patients whose families were in dire straits financially, and also for dozens of Muscular Dystrophy (Jerry Lewis) telethons for kids. I also did benefit concerts for SIDS (Sudden Infant Death Syndrome) and countless other needy charities. At one point I finally had to stop taking calls because the word was out – Danny Vann will come and do a concert for FREE for any charity around. It got to be too much and my bands complained that they needed to make money for their families. So we began filtering the requests and prioritizing. Children-focused charities took TOP priority. It was a dream-come-true for me to be able to help others like Elvis did with all his talent and money.

Now, I have a question for YOU. Who was your hero when you were growing up? How hard did you try to be like them? What happened to your dream? Are you still striving to be like them? Do you have a special gift that you never developed? Art? Music? Sports? Poetry? Writing? What if you picked that dream back up again and took it to a "higher" level? You see when you are doing what you LOVE – what you have a "passion" for - you are *not* working at it. You are fulfilling what God put you on earth for. You are completing yourself. We have each been made with a special gift – or even multiple gifts – consider these Bible passages to see more clearly:

> *Jeremiah 1:5* - Before I formed you in the belly I knew you; and before you came forth out of the womb I sanctified you, and I ordained you a prophet unto the nations.
>
> *2 Corinthians 4:6* - For it is the God who commanded light to shine out of darkness, who has shone in our hearts to give the light of the knowledge of the glory of God in the face of Jesus Christ. *7* But we have this

treasure in earthen vessels, that the excellency of the power may be of GOD, and not of us.

Romans 12:3 For I say, through the grace given to me, to everyone who is among you, not to think *of himself* more highly than he ought to think, but to think soberly, as God has dealt to each one a measure of faith. **4** For as we have many members in one body, but all the members do not have the same function, **5** so we, *being* many, are one body in Christ, and individually members of one another. **6** *Having then gifts differing according to the grace that is given to us, let us use them: if <u>prophecy</u>, let us prophesy in proportion to our faith;* **7** *or <u>ministry</u>, let us use it in our ministering; he who <u>teaches</u>, in teaching;* **8** *he who <u>exhorts</u>, in exhortation; he who <u>gives</u>, with liberality; he who <u>leads</u>, with diligence; he who shows <u>mercy</u>, with cheerfulness.*

When you finally realize why you are here, it's like coming back to the table after a long period of time and finally finding that lost piece of a jigsaw puzzle; or finding a restaurant that makes that special dish that tastes *exactly* like what grandma used to make. You longed for that taste for years after grandma died and then WOW, there it is.

I want to encourage you to search your soul and ask yourself, "Am I really doing what I LOVE to do?" If not, ask God to help you find a way to get back to it. Maybe you're just starting out and you took the first job that came along because the money was good. Maybe you're near retirement and you had no idea what to do with all your future free time. Maybe you had kids and had to lay your dream down for a few years. Or maybe you just got busy with life and making money to get all the things you thought would make you happy. Well, God is always there and waiting for you to turn your face toward Him and give Him glory and honor. When you follow His example, and turn from your distractions and/or bad ways (that is - to repent) – then you will have His ear and things will begin to turn around for you.

My Journey In The Shadow of "The King"
........From Graceland to the Promised Land

By doing what you LOVE, your light will begin to shine through. There will be a peace about you that others will not only notice, they will want to know how they can get it too. That's when you will have a chance to share Christ Jesus with them. Not necessarily with a sledge hammer like some of the Bible thumpers do...just let them know your story. Tell them how when you stopped chasing after all the worldly things and stopped running from God and looked at why and how he made you – your passion begin to surface. Share that once you stepped into your passion, everything began to fall into place.

I know I make it sound like it's so "easy." But truthfully, it's *not* really that *hard*. We bring a lot of struggles on ourselves by trying to please everybody else when God has already given us talents and desires. He knows why He made you. He knows what's best for you. When you fulfill those desires (or your calling) you honor Him. Then when you seek Him, He **will** answer. Do yourself a favor and start listening to your heart and doing what you know you should be doing. Then start trying to be like Him and watch what happens....

Look.....

I knew that in order to be taken seriously as an Elvis impersonator I needed to learn his songs. I knew that I better know all the words. I better know the music and it would help if I tried to look like him. In fact the first time I stepped on the stage with a white jumpsuit on *I* couldn't believe the difference in how I felt and how I presented myself. It was truly amazing. You might have experienced something like this when you dressed up in a Halloween costume as an adult some time; especially if you wore mask. You felt a unique freedom to act like your made-up character. I remember during the Gong Show years that there was a character called the "Unknown Comic". He wore a plain brown paper bag over his head with three holes in it; one for his mouth and two for his eyes. He was a real cut-up and quite popular at the time. Well I was performing at the Saginaw Moose for a Halloween Party and I didn't want people to know that I was there in the audience – or who I was when I first walked into the club. I got a brown paper bag and put it over my head. I never had so much fun as I did that night before show time. I was able to mingle in the audience and just cut-up and crack stupid jokes and really have a lot of fun and learn things about folks before the show.

Well, acting like Christ is really no different – except we don't have to grow long hair and a beard. (Isn't that a relief ladies?) We can conduct our lives like He did. We can be honest, gentle, loving, and kind. We don't even have to tell people that we are trying to be like Christ. We just do the things that we know He did. There was a saying that people should still use today – WWJD – What Would Jesus Do? If we all learned what Jesus did when he walked the earth and followed his example, that is if we imitated Him more often, our world would be a LOT better than it is today. In fact, I believe a more accurate phrase would be WDJD – What "Did" Jesus Do!

So let's do a quick review. How did I get to be so much like Elvis? I watched him very intently – very carefully – and repeatedly. How did I learn to be like Christ? I read about what He was like throughout the Bible and especially what He did in the New Testament and I watched movies about Him. How did I learn to sing like Elvis? I listened to him - over-and-over-and-over again. This also caused me to memorize the words and melodies of all his songs (he recorded over 700 of them by the way – and I know over 300). How did I learn to quote Jesus' words and actions? I read the Bible – over-and-over and over again. I talked about the things He did. I tried to do them myself and incorporate them into my daily routine. I intentionally worked at being like Him. And my life is SOOOO much better for it – really! There's a freedom in being honest and loving all the time.

No – I'm not perfect, I make mistakes. But, when my attitude became focused on honesty and love, my whole life was transformed. Just knowing that I was pleasing God and that He was watching and responding favorably to these changes has made it even more fulfilling. Things just keep getting better and better in my life.

This can happen for you too. I am praying for you; that our Heavenly Father will surround you with His loving arms and that you will feel His incredible LOVE. That you will have the courage and strength to truly act like, and become a son, or daughter, of the living, loving God of all creation. You will be so happy! Thank you Father! May **Your Will** be done! Amen!

My Journey In The Shadow of "The King"
........From Graceland to the Promised Land

Early in my entertainment career, as I was doing my "floor shows" and other special-event concerts, I began to notice a pattern emerging from the interactions I was having with the audiences. God was directing me to shake hands and give scarves and light-up roses to *certain* people that really needed a touch from God.

I know to some of you this is going to sound very weird, but there have been dozens and dozens of times when I would be drawn to a particular man or woman: where I would shake their hand, give them a scarf or one of my unique light-up silk roses. And to my complete surprise, they would come up to me after the show in tears and explain how they were widowed and their spouse loved the song *Love Me Tender* or *Can't Help Falling* or *In the Ghetto* – or some other song that I was singing at the time. They were moved because today was their wedding anniversary, birthday, or anniversary of their death. I came to them and helped them deal with their pain or loss. This has happened to me over-and-over-and-over again!

One woman said she saw an angel over my shoulder when I did her husband's favorite song during my performance – which was on his birthday! She was teary-eyed when she approached me and said, "God has truly blessed you with a great gift – never stop singing."

Others told me stories of how they miraculously were coerced into attending the concert against their will – only to be transformed and receive great joy and peace about some painful memory or loss that they had been praying to God for some help in dealing with for their situation.

The stories continue to come back to me even to this day of families healed of broken relationships and children having *good* memories of their parents (now deceased) who brought them to one of my concerts. Then, somehow out of an audience of several hundred people, I would select them and hold their hand, or sing their parent's favorite song and they would be filled with joy and peace.

You see, God is all Love and joy and peace. He is *not* the author of confusion and pain, because that is what Satan does to people. When God comes into a situation, the chaos stops. There is peace and clarity of vision. Joy reigns in the presence of our Almighty Creator. You don't see the planets spinning about the galaxy willy-nilly! No. There is order throughout creation. Things progress in what we call a *natural order* – but, in truth, God has ordered all things and is in constant control of all things!

Throughout my career I was surprised about how many of these incredible coincidences happened to me. But, now that I have extensively studied the Bible, and sat at the feet of many Bible scholars and preachers, I understand that *nothing* happens without His order (Job 1:10) and *"the very hairs of your head are all numbered"* (Matthew 10:30 and 1 Samuel 14:45). God knows the plans he has for each of us – *"Plans to prosper us – not to harm us"* (Jeremiah 29:11). So start looking – and expecting – for God to move into all of the situations in YOUR life. Ask Him what He wants you to learn from things that happen to you. Don't challenge Him and ask Him "why" He's doing something to you – TRUST Him. Believe that He always has your best interest in mind.

His Word (the Bible) tells us, *"All things work toward the good of those called to His purpose"* (Romans 8:28). That means even the smallest detail, like combing your hair works toward the ultimate goal of God's plan for your life. I know this is probably hard for some of you to believe; but our creator – the God of the entire cosmos with its billions upon billions of galaxies each containing billions and billions of stars - cares about you combing your hair. Well, I'm here to tell you that according to His own words – in the Bible - YES HE DOES!!! He cares about every breath you take. Just like a new mother listens to every breath her newborn baby takes while the baby sleeps at night. *That* is how attentive God is to *your* breathing and every activity that you do.

WHOA! Do you mean God is listening to EVERY breath, word, and every thought that I have – EVERYDAY?

YES HE DOES! And He wants the best for each of us! That's why He will place people like you and me in the path of another person that needs something that we have to give to them in their time of need. Sometimes it's as simple as a glass of water, a bag of chips, a scarf, a pair of mittens, maybe just a simple smile, or other random act of kindness. When you are there for someone else, you are serving God. This was one of the primary messages Jesus delivered to mankind. He said it was a "new commandment" (John 13:34) "*A new commandment I give you, Love one another as I have loved you.*" And He also said that ALL the law and ALL the commandments are fulfilled when we give love: "*'You shall love the Lord your God with all your heart, with all your soul, and with all your mind.' This is the first and great commandment. And the second is like it: 'You shall love your neighbor as yourself.' On these two commandments hang all the Law and the Prophets.*" (Matthew 22:36-40).

When we look at the Messiah's life and all of the actions He took, and the miracles He performed for various people, we see how God wants us to live and act toward one another. God came to earth in the flesh of Jesus to show us what a perfect man would live like and how we should treat each other. If you want to know how to treat somebody in a certain situation, pick up your Bible and read about what Jesus and His followers did under similar circumstances.

These things that have happened to me over the years have opened my eyes to see all the good things that God is using the musical gifts and talents that He gave to me and ultimately made me for. I give Him all the Glory. He gave me the voice, the Elvis looks, talents, and the opportunities. I am happy to serve Him in song and any other way He needs me to.

My prayer for you is that you will also discover what God made you for, and begin to serve others as He presents various opportunities to you. It's really not that hard. Just be open to situations where you can be kind and generous. Watch for people that are in need as you go through your day. It could be a person sobbing in a hallway, or a beggar on the street, or a lonely widow down the block standing at her window as you pass by. Be *looking* for ways to serve God. I pray personally every morning that God will use me to His glory that day. Sometimes it's just that simple – ask and you shall receive. What are YOU asking for? Is it always something for yourself – or do you ask Him to use you to help others? Start giving to others and watch what happens in return to you.

My Journey In The Shadow of "The King"
........From Graceland to the Promised Land

One of the many benefits that have emerged from writing this book was a new level of communication and understanding between my son Troy and me. The following is his reflection on the events that impacted his life…

When my Dad first told me that he was writing a book about his life/journey, I was intrigued to finally see his first-hand account of the events which had shaped his life. Somewhere in the course of perusing and discussing the first few drafts, he and I had a conversation that encompassed *my* feelings and actions following his first bypass surgery. Allow me to add some context:

It was 1998 and I had been a Marine Corps Infantryman for two years. The relationship between my father and I had become….tenuous, at best. I had heard so much of my Mom's side of the divorce story, and the evil Step-Mother had lived up to the stereotype enough for me to decide to, "opt out" if you will, from hearing or dealing with anything else. I was sick of all of the drama from this, the final chapter of my high-school years, and I was writing my own book a half-a-country (and sometimes world) away. I really felt that I didn't need this hassle, and I shut my Dad out.

Upon hearing of his bypass surgery, it finally hit me hard that I could have easily lost my father, and the baggage I was carrying was years old. I started wondering how that could have felt if I had held that grudge until the end. I didn't like where my imagination took me.

It didn't take long for me to reach out, and although I had to set some ground rules (I was absolutely insistent about refusing to hear anything negative about one parent from the other), we made great strides reconnecting. I realized that I needed my father in my life, despite any perceived or realized misgivings from our past.

The moral of this story is simple: Life is short. Don't hold grudges against those you love, because you never know how much time you have left with them. In the end, it's just not worth it. I am nowhere near perfect, and neither is my relationship with my family or its many branches. And yet, despite this, I firmly believe that if I died today, those most important to me would know how much love I had for them. To this day, I regularly speak to both of my parents and my only sibling, and I pray to God that I can instill the importance of maintaining these relationships to my own children.

I hate to preach to anyone about how to live their lives, as I'm not the most exemplary, upstanding Christian by any standard, but I promise that if you can find forgiveness in your heart and maintain even a modicum of decency and love for your family, you will die with one less regret. Honestly, you might even change the life of someone you love for the better in the process.

It took me 21 years to realize the importance of this story, and my Dad thought it was relevant enough to add to *his* book. I am both humbled and honored to be given the opportunity to add my insight, and I only hope that these words do it justice.

God bless,

Troy J. Van Pelt

My Journey In The Shadow of "The King"
........From Graceland to the Promised Land

Music Library – Songs in this book

I Hear an Angel Whispering
Gimme-a-Hug
Grandma's Song Intro
Grandma's Song - Ode to Josie
In His Arms
Road Rage Song
Enchanted
All My Burdens
Be Healed
Feel the Joy
God is Everywhere

BONUS:
How Great Thou Art (Danny's interpretation - sung Elvis style)
Amazing Grace (Danny's interpretation - sung Elvis style)
Jesus – (by Jayden Leaman – one of Danny's favorites!)

These songs may be found at: www.Broadjam.com/DannyVann

My Journey In The Shadow of "The King"
........From Graceland to the Promised Land

Bibliography

All Bible quotes are from BibleStudyTools.com the New King James version unless otherwise noted

Lake Mitchell and Lake Cadillac. When winter sets in, the channel immediately freezes over until the lakes freeze. Then the channel opens up and no matter how cold it gets outside, the channel never freezes over again! It is one of the most unusual wonders of the world. (http://upnorthmichigan.com/Wonders/CadillacCanal.aspx)

Most things were from magazines, but the story that I remembered the most was about how he experimented with his own dancing style. He said he would wiggle his leg and the girls went wild. His manager told him; go out and do it again (http://mentalfloss.com/article/30282/elvis-presleys-strangest-concert) http://www.elvis.net/facts/factsframe.html

It has been said that unforgiveness is like taking poison and then waiting for the OTHER person to die. How crazy is that? https://www.brainyquote.com/quotes/marianne_williamson_635346 ...author unknown?

I saw a night shirt at a gift shop that said "When you go to sleep at night, give your problems to God. He's up all night anyway."

Abe Lincoln: "To ease another's heartache is to forget one's own." https://www.motivationalwellbeing.com/55-meaningful-quotes-about-helping-others.html

Made in the USA
San Bernardino, CA
11 August 2019